"With a deep biblical commitment, a firm grasp of the power of the parable, and a profound insight into the complexities of the twenty-first century Christian woman, Chaffee guides us on a journey of self-discovery. She encourages us to see the reflection of ourselves in the parables of Christ and to integrate his timely teachings into the myriad of roles we enact in everyday life."

— Susan A. Carter, Ph.D.,
Assistant Professor of Psychology, Lee University

❧

"This book will change lives because it requires us to peer into a mirror where we not only see ourselves but the very image of God. Janice skillfully holds up the parabolic mirror where revelation and restoration await those who dare to take an unflinching look. You just might be surprised at what you'll see!"

— Kathy Mainse, Television co-host of
"100 Huntley Street," Ontario, Canada

❧

"Sometimes it takes a powerful, objective observer to force us to look within. This is what I experienced while reading this book. It is a well-written, thought-provoking tool for spiritual inquiry."

— Hattie Winston, Actress on the television show *Becker*,
Singer/Producer/Director

❧

"Janice delivers captivating and updated, yet theological and well-developed, parables for the modern woman with thoughtful, direct, yet gentle, writing. She weaves the reader into the story, causing self-examination of Christian character."

— Jan Wyder, Director of Women's Ministries
Grace Church, Eden Prairie, Minnesota

❧

"*If the Prodigal Were a Daughter* is a beautifully written book that brings new and fresh insight to women. It allows us to see ourselves for who we are and who we can become in Christ."

— Michelle Cavinder, Director of Women's Ministries
Crystal Cathedral, Garden Grove, California

❧

"What Janice has done to advance God's Kingdom is extraordinary. Women and men from all around the world will see themselves in a whole new light as they read story after story of God's unchanging power. The characters may be different, but Janice makes it clear there is no denying that the truths of scripture are the same yesterday, today, and for all eternity."

— Leesa Bellesi, Co-Author of *The Kingdom Assignment*
Pastor's Wife, Speaker

❧

"When was the last time you looked in the mirror and saw the reflection of Christ? If you're looking for a volt of lightening to jolt your spiritual attitude and consciousness, read this book and be revived."

— Rev. Yvonne McCoy, Pastor of Women and Spiritual Growth
Colorado Community Church, Englewood, Colorado

"If the Prodigal Were a Daughter was fun and touching and relatable...I mused on it for days. God has given Janice a tremendous talent and will use this book to accomplish his purpose. Gracias Señor, que Usted va hablar por las páginas de este libro."
— Pastor Vangie Gonzales
King of Glory Assembly of God, Austin, Texas

❧

"This is a brilliant insight into the human condition. Each story is an invitation to think, to feel, to study and understand what it means to reflect the image of God."
— Rev. Care Crawford, Pastor of Family Ministries
Bel Air Presbyterian Church, Los Angeles, California

❧

"The retold parable is extremely vivid and imaginative, but my favorite part is the well-researched analysis. The personal application section really hits the target, and a parable that you've always skimmed over becomes impossible to ignore."
— Tanya Streder, Operations Manager
K-LIFE Radio (KLFF-FM) San Luis Obispo, California

❧

"Janice's approach to the parables grabs and holds my attention. She leaves no stone unturned while painting each character thoroughly, revealing their heart's intentions. Her beautiful writing style captured me and I left her work realizing that regardless of our position in life, God has called us to serve."
— Jan Marshall, Shepherd's Door Ministry to Women and their
Children, Portland Rescue Mission

❧

"Storytelling is Janice's strength, and you'll find it difficult to put down her book. Just as Jesus used the stories of everyday lives, Janice uncovers layer by layer our own lives through the lens of a woman's perspective. The refreshing look at the spiritual truths in these parables provides us with tools for discussion in order to probe the impact they have in our lives."
— Mary Pandiani, Director of Women's Ministries
Chapel Hill Presbyterian Church, Gig Harbor, Washington

❧

"Janice is a masterful wordsmith! With vivid descriptions and captivating story lines, these parables provide soul-searching personal application. The questions that follow each chapter trigger choices that will produce positive change. If you have a prodigal daughter or if you've ever been one, read this book!"
— Carol Kent, International Speaker, Author
President, Speak Up Speaker Services

❧

"Janice has captured my attention and my heart with her modern day formatting of the parables of the Bible. Women in starring roles! I like that! Her storytelling capabilities are magnificent and who doesn't love a good story? The study guide made it easy to move beyond the story and figure out how it applies to me today, and to examine my own life in light of scripture."
— Sue Buchanan, Author, Speaker

JANICE CHAFFEE

If the Prodigal Were a Daughter

HARVEST HOUSE™ PUBLISHERS

EUGENE, OREGON

Cover design by Koechel Peterson & Associates, Inc., Minneapolis, Minnesota

IF THE PRODIGAL WERE A DAUGHTER
Copyright © 2003 by Janice Chaffee
Published by Harvest House Publishers
Eugene, Oregon 97402

ISBN 0-7394-3189-7

For Teresa Spurlock
and
Rev. Rebecca Ferrell Nickel
and their ever-widening
community of God's people

Acknowledgments

Terry Glaspey at Harvest House did for me what every good editor does: convinced the author to rewrite. I owe him thanks for editing my work and encouraging me with enthusiasm. Hope Lyda edited with precision, and filled our conversations with great humor, sensitivity, and care, for which I am grateful.

Many friends and associates contributed essential information. My sincere thanks to Karen Clark, First Vice President at Sun Trust Bank, who clarified financial terms, and to Kelly Ford who gave valuable insights on homeschooling.

My appreciation goes to Paul and Elizabeth McCusker, the first ones to read a draft of the prodigal parable, for their helpful comments and opinions. I am indebted to Dwight Ozard, whose thought-provoking comments prompted me to ask the "tough" questions. He's still witty and devout after a year of battling cancer, and the e-mails he sent during his time of treatment were parables of faith and hope.

I love Craig Ellsworth as a brother. His support of me and this book never wavered. No one in the world is as creative as David Nickel, and the menu he helped prepare for the banquet parable is just a sampling of his culinary flair. The International Food Club feeds my soul with as much spice and flavor as the dishes set on the tables. Thank you for the honor of feasting in your company.

I am grateful to a great variety of women around the country who listened as I merged parables with fictional stories and with stories from my own life. Their responses helped shape the final form of this book.

Special thanks go to Gail Hamilton Masondo for the privilege of once again telling her story. She is the sister of my soul. My gratitude is also extended to the unnamed women whose disguised but true stories I have been trusted to use.

Barbara Roberts Pine remains my editor, my mentor, and my friend. I can only hope to repay my indebtedness to her by helping someone else with the same sacrificial attention she has given me.

My husband, Jim, read every page after every edit, consoled my frustration, and cheered my progress. His devotion to me and our sons is a living parable of unconditional love.

Contents

Introduction

Almost everyone knows the plot of the Prodigal Son parable. A rich kid left his family, squandered his inheritance in a foreign land, and ended up wallowing in a pigsty. Destitute and near death, he got up and went home, where his loving father met him with open arms, and they lived happily ever after.

This ancient story is good and exemplary for boys. But what about girls? What is the modern story of a Prodigal Daughter?

I picture her as an honor-roll high-school graduate turned wild party-girl expelled from college. Abandoned by her first love after an abortion, she sedated herself in a downward spiral of alcohol, drugs, and promiscuity. She bounced from one job to another, had an affair with a married man, and then left the country to escape disappointment and loss. Years later, lonely, weak from an eating disorder, and painfully aware of her emotional, physical, and spiritual bankruptcy, she returned to her father's home to ask for forgiveness.

Parts of her story belong to me and to many other women because we see aspects of her every time we look in the mirror. Or, we see who she has become. With or without the specific details, most of us identify with her desire for love, her musing on what might have been, her remorse for foolish decisions, her hope for a "happily ever after" ending.

The universal power of the prodigal parable is truth. It accurately portrays youthful flight from family and from faith. It shows the worry and fears of a parent agonizing over a lost child. And it offers hope of redemption and reconciliation.

Throughout history, many storytelling styles were fashioned to impart truth. Oral tradition must have begun when Adam and Eve warmed their hands by a fire and reminisced about their evening strolls with God and their calamitous conversation with a snake. I imagine their wide-eyed children, faces flushed and warm from the crackling flames, awed by the story of a talking serpent.

At some point in the development of human culture, story-telling evolved from fact to fiction. What circumstances led a wise person to contrive a story as a creative form for pre-senting truth? By the year 600 B.C., Aesop collected and wrote fables using animated plants and animals to illustrate moral principles. Later, fairy tales used heroes and heroines, magic and disguise to preserve the history and culture of countries, rulers, and subjects. Myths cleverly explained the origins of created things and the exploits of gods and humans. The pur-pose of such fiction was remarkably grasped by a five-year-old girl as "stories that aren't true on the outside, but they are true on the inside!"[1]

Parables, however, intentionally add another element to storytelling. They merge truth and fiction with the reality of God. They blend the matter of fact with the mystery of faith. They are stories for the soul. The literal meaning of *parabolē* is "something cast along side, side-throwing." The storyteller throws a fictional situation alongside the life of a listener.

Jesus has been called the greatest Storyteller of all time. Amazingly, one-third of his recorded words are in parabolic form. Why such a prolific use of fiction? Because first-century listeners, specifically members of his own Jewish culture and community, were familiar with the purpose of these mini-dramas. They knew that parables required them to identify with at least one of the characters in the story, required them to choose the character which best represented their own atti-tudes, behaviors, and actions.

Jesus' parables are like a two-sided mirror. In one side, we see a reflection of ourselves. We see that the issues and struggles confronting the fictional characters parallel our own. A look at their lives gives us an opportunity to clearly see ourselves. Initially we may not think it possible, but each of us is represented, regardless of how we differ in gender, age, or race, or by denomination, social status, or experience.

On the other side of the parable mirror, we see a reflection of God. The fictional character representing God shatters previous portrayals of "Yahweh" as a harsh judge, a vengeful warrior, a requirer of sacrifice. Jesus enlarged the image to show a caring, more compassionate Deity. In his stories, God is seen as a tender parent, a just friend, a lavish giver of grace.

Questions were implicit at the end of a parable, whether or not verbally asked. Jesus expected the listeners, both past and present, to ask themselves, "Am I like that man, that woman? Do I do those things, treat people in that manner, react to others in that way?" The final question is paramount: "Will I reject the application or will I change as a result of hearing it?" Personal response sets a parable apart from other forms of fiction. Parables are not merely lessons, they are not histories, they are not moral principles. They are challenges meant to cause change. Once we determine who we are, Jesus presents the alternative of who we can become—a reflection of God.

The power of a biblical parable was established from the very first recorded in the Old Testament.[2] A prophet named Nathan used story as an indictment against King David's moral failure and religious disobedience. The condensed version is this: David woke up from an afternoon nap, took a stroll on his rooftop garden, and spied upon a bathing beauty. The woman was the wife of one of his generals who happened to be away at war. Indulging his power and lust, David had Bathsheba brought to his bed chamber for a sexual tryst, then sent her back home. Later, when Bathsheba notified David of her pregnancy, the king solved the problem of scandal by having her husband killed and by returning the widow to the palace for a hasty wedding. Outraged by the king's actions, Nathan appeared before the throne to tell a story. Who can take offense at a nice story? That seems to have been the attitude of David when Nathan began, "There once was..." The king leaned forward with unsuspecting attention.

"There once was a rich man," said Nathan. David nodded with understanding; he, too, was very rich. "And there was a poor man," Nathan continued, "a poor man who owned nothing but one little ewe lamb that had been raised as a member of the man's family." David understood. He once had been a shepherd and knew the love and devotion for a precious lamb.

"The little ewe," said Nathan, verbally painting a pastoral scene, "shared the poor man's food, drank from his cup, and even slept in his arms. She was like a daughter to him. When the rich man wanted to prepare a feast for his guest, he did not take a lamb from his own herd. No, he slaughtered the poor man's lamb for the evening meal."

"Dear God!" shouted the king who jumped to his feet in righteous indignation. Spluttering with anger, David swore that the man who did such a thing deserved to die, because of his lack of pity. You can bet that had this been a true account, the rich man's head would have been on a stick within the hour. But there was no rich man. This was a parable.

"You are the man," Nathan pointed his finger at the king. "You are the man." The prophet threw the story alongside perfectly. Why did Nathan use fictional characters in a setting so familiar to David? The answer is obvious. David needed to see a reflection of himself, a clear picture of his injustice. Until Nathan's story, David had not faced the responsibility of his actions. Why parable? It mirrored the rift between his behavior and the expectations of God.

A thousand or so years later, when Jesus was a boy, parables were prominent in Jewish tradition. He heard them in the synagogue and at his father's side, or even in the open air, as rabbis often taught outdoors, setting their stories in the surroundings of the open fields or seashores. When Jesus was an adult and began to teach his own followers, parable was his favorite means of presenting a divine perspective on life. His stories simplified the complexities of religious and daily experience, and they required a reaction.

How do we respond, these thousands of years later? Do we, like a Lost Boy in *Peter Pan,* ask, "Am I in this story?" Do we glimpse our reflection in the mirror thrown alongside us? Do we see our own conduct in the characters that appear in the dramas of Jesus?

King David's reaction to Nathan's parable is a great story in itself. I noticed that his identification with the wealthy character required one of three responses. The first was adamant denial. He could have heartily laughed or indignantly roared with innocence and added lying to his list of sins. His second choice, defensive avoidance, would have shifted the burden of proof to his accuser and justified sentencing Nathan to death. The third option, acknowledgment of truth, was a precursor to repentance and forgiveness. Fortunately, he chose well and set a timeless example.

At the conclusion of Jesus' parables, each one of us, like David, is required to choose one of these three options. In spite of the fact that his stories were told a long time ago, in a land far away, the purpose remains the same. We are to recognize ourselves, then respond.

When I was a flower child in the late '60s and early '70s, I was unaware of Nathan's story, of David's options. I didn't know Jesus' parable about a discontent teenager paralleled my life. I didn't know that social freedoms of my contemporary culture had personal repercussions. I denied responsibility for my unhappy existence by blaming others and avoided facing truth by literally flying to a foreign country.

Unless we intentionally deceive ourselves, truth will find us all, whether we live in a palace or pigsty, at home or abroad. When it does, whether we hang from the brink of spiritual or physical death, we are forced to make a choice. Once our choice is made, the stories shift, our lives change. If we choose well, following the example of David and the prodigal, we begin the process of maturity.

My prodigal story ended with restoration, forgiveness, and a new direction. Even as I write this, it's hard for me to believe the girl I once was found grace to begin again, grow up, change, and mature into womanhood.

Jesus constantly presented truth to his followers for the sake of their maturity: the truth of his own life, the truth of God, the truth of human nature modeled by the characters in his stories. It amazes me how relevant his parables are these centuries later. They pierce through our present social structure and through our religious, political, public, and personal lives.

I wrote this book for people who want to understand the presence of Jesus in the first century and in the twenty-first. It is for those willing to take an unflinching look at their own image in the parabolic mirror.

In *Hamlet,* Shakespeare told his actors that they, as players, were to hold "the mirror up to nature, to show virtue her own feature." Jesus tells us to look into the parable to see our own reflection and a reflection of God.

As I wrote *If the Prodigal Were a Daughter,* my hope was that by retelling the stories in a modern setting with a mostly female cast, the reader might hear the parables as if for the first time. The updated versions are followed by the original Scriptures and a look at the historical context to see how the parables applied to the original hearers and, in turn, how they apply to us.

I included stories from my life and from the lives of women I know to illustrate that it "is not we who explain the parable; rather, it is the parable which explains us."[3] Parables are not improbable accounts of unusual people, but are accurate depictions of ordinary life. Personal stories reinforce the reflective truth.

Like those who first heard Jesus speak, readers may be surprised by the exactness of these simple plots, the pertinence of the conflicts, and the familiarity of the players. The intention of these stories thrown alongside us is to cause recognition of our motives and our character. And, as seen in the examples of King David and of the prodigal, the result is a changed life. I know. My life changed when I recognized myself as a prodigal daughter and made the decision to come home. As I write in the last chapter, years later I recognized myself in yet another character, and my life changed again. My hope is that once you see your reflection in the parable mirror, you, too, will welcome the possibility of a new image.

Welcome to the power of a parable.

The Image
of Compassion

Sammi: An Unlikely Neighbor

❦

The Waiting

*What I mean by living to one's self is living in
the world, as in it, not of it...
It is to be a silent spectator of the mighty scene of things...
to take a thoughtful, anxious interest or curiosity
in what is passing in the world,
but not to feel the slightest inclination to make or
meddle with it.*
—WILLIAM HAZLITT, 1778–1830

*Truth is one forever absolute,
but opinion is truth filtered through the moods,
the blood, the disposition of the spectator.*
—WENDELL PHILLIPS, 1811–1884

Shelby stretched her legs against the floorboard and locked her arms against the steering wheel. She plopped her head against the headrest and stared through half-open eyes at a dark neon sign, willing its cursive OPEN to ignite. Why a coffee shop was still closed at six in the morning was beyond comprehension, too much to consider without her usual first cup of coffee. The wood-shingled diner attached to a shabby motel was a clue not to expect anything fancy from Sissy's Country Kitchen. *This early in the day,* Shelby thought, *I'd welcome hot, dark water.*

She yawned in the darkness and watched the sunrise, not all that thrilling for a night owl, especially not today. No orange or magenta streaks in the heavens, no candy pink swirls, just continuous ribs of nickel gray. Maybe this was an omen. Cloudy morning, late opening restaurant, no sign of the Love entourage. She assumed her coverage of the Power of Love Conference would be a perfunctory no-brainer: show up early, take posed photos, snap some audience responses, write down names of women giddy at the prospect of being quoted, go home, write a flattering story, e-mail it to the religion editor at the paper, and call it a day. There would be no surprises covering the founder and main attraction of the Love conventions. There was nothing new to write about Reverend Rachel Lovden.

It was common tabloid knowledge that Rachel worked her way through seminary as a runway model. She had married a gorgeous architect, and together they had produced two perfectly adorable daughters. Her installation as the first female pastor of Kansas' largest interdenominational church captured the local headlines for a week. The accompanying articles characterized her life as a modern-day fairy tale, a story of success and failure, of accomplishment and addiction to little green pills. The modeling agency's doctor had kept their petite star well supplied with uppers—pea-sized insurance against weight gain. The five-foot, three-inch, 92-pound Rachel justified popping speed with her workload: attend classes by day, pose for print ads in the afternoon, study Greek and Hebrew by night, strut runways on the weekends. She reasoned that the tiny tablets were like vitamins, a little something extra to keep her healthy and energetic—until her heart started to beat erratically, until her breath held the tinge of death, until her skin hung loose on her bones. Until she checked herself into the hospital. Years later, she told thousands of women who flocked to her seminars that she conquered her addiction with the power of love: love of life, love of her husband, love of her God.

Shelby had verified all the details of Rachel's biography and read every available story on the phenomenon of religious celebrity, from the popular pope to Kathie Lee to Jesse Jackson. With journalistic cynicism, she skipped over all the theological jargon and religious lingo littering each piece. Shelby wanted to know what *really* motivated them, what fed their desire to stand in the spotlight, why they parroted clichés and thanked God or Jesus every time a microphone was in front of their face.

Rachel was just a young, newer version of the old, big-haired television evangelists, Shelby believed; a slick performer with the same insatiable need to stand in the center of attention. Religiosity was just another performance art, even while demurely giving credit to a higher power.

Still, the incongruity of Rachel's physical beauty and spiritual devotion, a cross between Courtney Cox and Mother Teresa, was captivating. The feminine pastor charmed the press with her honesty and took advantage of every occasion to preach to a captive audience. Shelby knew, in the dawning day, that she would not be exempt from Rachel's "Power of Love" assault. An involuntary smile pulled at her lips. Early morning or not, she was eager to meet the woman whose image graced both the covers of *People* magazine and *Modern Christian Women*. Maybe she would find a new angle on the famous Rev. Rachel.

The pre-dawn shift from flat black to pearly gray seemed to take forever. Shelby bounced her leg and tapped her fingers. She fidgeted with her camera and focused on the restaurant window. Kitchen lights seemed to be on. *Why aren't they open?* she thought. *Is anybody in there?*

As if signaled, the OPEN sign spluttered to life and the vibrant pink neon fuzzed in the lens. Shelby winced but held the camera steady, the auto-focus locked on a plump woman bound by a white apron. The waitress unlocked the front door, then quickly retreated past red vinyl seats and white Formica table tops.

Finally, Shelby tisked. She put her Nikon back in the case on the passenger seat just as a beam of headlights flashed across the parking lot. A large Mercedes maneuvered into a space about thirty feet from the restaurant door. Shelby instinctively picked up her camera, never taking her eyes off the car. *Wonder if Rachel's driving,* she thought.

The Conflict

There are two tragedies in life.
One is to lose your heart's desire.
The other is to gain it.
—GEORGE BERNARD SHAW, 1856–1950

Rachel turned off the engine and lifted her foot from the brake pedal. The pre-dawn drive had been an emotionally dark journey through a lonely landscape. Parked at her destination, she made no attempt to get out of the car. *I feel safer in here than anyplace else,* she sighed. She flipped down the visor mirror. Her well-maintained exterior, seen and adored by so many, was a thin shell, one she feared would shatter at any moment. She slapped the mirror closed. *What is happening to me?*

Unanswerable questions skittered through her mind. *How can I admit the dichotomy of wanting it all and wanting to walk away? How can I keep standing under pressure strong enough to leave bruises?* Certain aspects of her life, Rachel admitted, were undeniably fabulous, but some were hairline cracks threatening to become fissures. Not even the power of love could hold her together much longer.

Her eyes swept across the aging two-story conference center next to the cheap restaurant and run-down motel. The modern 1960s architecture now looked dated and dingy. She made a mental note: *Tell Faith never to book another small-town auditorium.* It just wasn't worth the trouble for only 2000 women. Faith's predictable response rang in her ears: *But it's good local publicity, especially in your own state. And it shows you are willing to go wherever you're asked. This will be the last small venue, I promise.* But in a year or so, Faith would add another gratuitous event to Rachel's schedule.

Rachel smiled at the mental image of Faith Vestry, the organizer of her life, the coordinator of her every move. Faith's capabilities as a volunteer at one of the fledgling Power of Love Conferences so impressed Rachel that she instinctively hired her on the spot. It proved to be one of her best decisions. Faith's control of the minutiae was the means that moved Rachel from attentive audiences of 250 to ecstatic crowds of 10,000.

Faith controlled Rachel's schedule, accepting or declining daily requests for photo sessions and private interviews, invitations from writer's groups and speaking conferences, in addition to book signings and special appearances. Just this week Faith began negotiations for Rachel to host a Sunday morning religious segment on a prominent network news show. The upside: national exposure would elevate Rachel's profile and expand her outreach. The downside: it was one more thing in an already hectic life.

Rachel sighed again. She was grateful for all these opportunities and she certainly didn't mean to complain. But she was sinking in a swamp of commitments. She missed sleeping at home with her husband. At least three nights a week, she crawled alone between stiff hotel sheets. She missed having the girls with her; the nights of giggling, shared bubble baths, the thrill of room service. Her babies were growing up and couldn't travel with her anymore because of school. *I'll make up for it when I'm home,* Rachel convinced herself. But when she tried to jump in and be a part of the action, young eyes told her she was in the way, a near outsider. The only place Rachel felt secure was on the stage, where adoring eyes welcomed and revered her. *When did this happen?* she wondered. *How did it get so twisted that the office can't run without me and home runs better without me?*

I should get out of this business. It's too exhausting. Why, she asked herself, *did God allow me to suceed if the price was going to be so high?* She felt like an innocent bystander trapped by the swell of her own press. All she did was tell her story, first in women's meetings, then at community Bible studies and youth groups. Someone typed up a one-page press release and sent it out to local churches. As word of her "pious effervescence" spread (how she *hated* that phrase), invitations to speak in nearby cities poured in. Before she knew it, she was booked on cable talk shows, pictured in magazine articles, reviewed in the religious section of newspapers. Overwhelmed by growing national attention and frustrated by the lack of time to properly prepare her Sunday sermons, Rachel submitted a letter of resignation to her church. But the congregation would not accept it; they were so proud of "our" Rev. Rachel.

I'm scared, Rachel admitted. Sunlight glared off the hood of her car. *I'm scared this is becoming another addiction. I know fame won't last forever, but this may be over before I'm ready to let it go.* Her sincere vow to serve God on the public stage as long as her message was pertinent now seemed immature and irrelevant. *Oh, God,* she prayed, *how do I stay real in such an unreal place? How do I balance home and career, life and ministry, taking care of myself, and obedience to Your call?* Rachel gripped the steering wheel. *God, what do You want from me? If this is what I'm supposed to be doing, why do I feel like I'm being destroyed?*

No answer came. She sat for several minutes and then took the keys out of the ignition and stepped out of the car. *Focus,* she advised herself. *Stay focused on what today requires of me and let Faith and the staff handle the other stuff. Separate work from life.* Rachel shook her head in despair. *Isn't faith in God supposed to permeate work and life? Aren't they inseparable? Why do these areas of my life feel so divided?*

Rachel's self-analysis and theological postulating only added more pressure. The woman with the answers had none for herself. With another deep sigh, she locked the car with her remote and headed toward the door of Sissy's Country Kitchen.

The Discovery

In completing one discovery
we never fail to get an imperfect knowledge of others
of which we could have no idea before,
so that we cannot solve one doubt without creating
several new ones.
—JOSEPH PRIESTLEY, 1733–1804

Steam rose from the dewy asphalt. *It's going to be a sunny day after all,* Shelby decided. She and the light meter were ready when Rachel's size six heels hit the sidewalk. *Click.* A curvaceous figure hardly concealed by a short-skirted navy suit hurried toward the door. *Click.* Glossy black hair bounced with every step. *Click.* Stunning green eyes. *Click.*

Rachel slowed midway between her car and the glass doors. Twisting her head inquisitively, she stepped off the sidewalk, bent slightly as if inspecting something on the ground. Then in one almost-comical motion, she leapt back like a startled kitten. Puzzled by such odd behavior, Shelby adjusted the lens to see what Rachel saw. Something blurred in the viewfinder. She switched to manual focus. *Holy Moly!* A naked woman sprawled between two ornamental bushes. Early dawn shadows had kept her hidden, but the morning light exposed her motionless, nude body. Shelby's reporter mode sprung into action. She widened the frame to capture both women. *Click.* The automatic forward whined with each successive shot. *Who is that woman? What is Rachel going to do?*

Rachel's knees wobbled as she stepped backwards onto the cement, staring at the supine woman. *Oh, God, this is horrible. I can't handle this. It's too much. I have to speak today and meet and sign and…it's just so unending. If I get off schedule, my whole day will be ruined and I won't get home in time to be with the girls after school. Oh Lord, how can this be happening to me? If I report this, I'll have to wait here, and my day is already crammed.* Rachel's hands pulled on her jacket lapels. *This isn't my problem,* she insisted. *I only wanted a cup of coffee. I don't have time for this.*

A gust of wind rearranged Rachel's hair over her face, but the image of the naked body burned in her eyes like a reverse negative. *How does a woman wind up in this predicament?* She squinted between fluttering strands to see if the woman was dead. Suddenly, she didn't want to know. *I can't get involved. I have two thousand other women to take care of today. Let someone else do it. If Faith were here, she would know what to do. Faith.* Rachel scanned the parking lot for a beige Volvo. For the first time, Faith was late for their pre-conference coffee. *I'll let Faith handle this,* she decided.

Straightening her spine, Rachel took several large strides back toward her car, unlocked the doors with the remote, pulled the handle and jumped inside. She was unaware of the first and the last *click.*

Shelby couldn't believe her eyes. Did Rachel just ignore a dead woman? *Maybe she went for help.* Zooming in on the deceased, now radiant in the morning sunshine, Shelby saw deep gashes crusted with blood, bruises in irregular shapes, arms and legs bent at wrong angles. It was impossible to guess her age or ethnicity. Shelby lingered on the woman's knuckled fists, clenched as if still fighting off her attackers.

The shutter opened and closed as rapidly as the questions flashed across Shelby's mind. *Who is she? How did she get there? Who did this to her? Why hadn't I noticed her before? Why didn't Rachel do something? Where did she go?*

Ingrained habits caused the photojournalist to automatically take out the exposed film and drop in a new roll. *Good Lord, someone needs to do something.* She looked up as a beige Volvo station wagon pulled in.

The Second Discovery

What you see and hear
depends a good deal on where you are standing:
it also depends on what sort of person you are.
—C. S. LEWIS, 1898–1963

The highest possible stage in moral culture
is when we recognize that we ought to control our thoughts.
—CHARLES ROBERT DARWIN, 1809–1882

Faith didn't need a printout anymore. The checklist was permanently etched in her mind. Call FedEx tracking to make sure the boxes had been delivered; call the auditorium manager to make sure they had been received; load Rachel's motivational tapes in the back of her station wagon; pack a box with extra batteries, a backup lavaliere, a duplicate video. She was prepared for any possible emergency in pulling off a Power of Love Conference. On the day of the event, Faith was calm. She knew that two buses transporting fifty eager volunteers would arrive at the venue by 7:45 A.M. A select few would unpack and display Rachel's books and tapes on tables stationed next to every door leading into the auditorium. No one could enter or exit without passing stacks of Rev. Rachel's resources. Faith made sure of it.

There was no deviation from the schedule in Faith's dominion. Everything was orderly and occurred on time. The musicians' sound check started precisely at 7:30. Main doors opened at 8:30 and the praise team started the conference at 9:00. Then Rev. Rachel entered and spoke for an hour. A thirty-minute intermission gave the women time for a potty break and for a buying frenzy at the product tables. Lively music lured the crowd back for Rachel's second message, which ended around noon. The program was the same, no matter the city or auditorium or number of women attending. Clockwork.

Caterers delivered lunch in the green room by 11:45 and cleared out leftovers by 1:15. Then, the big finale. Musicians rallied the crowd to their feet to prevent after-lunch drowsiness and drummed up emotion with rousing repetitions of peppy choruses. Once the audience was sufficiently hyped, the lights dimmed and a large screen descended for a twelve-minute video on Rachel's life and ministry. Next came Faith's favorite part. Before giving the signal for the lights to come back up, Rachel took her stance in the middle of the dark stage. Someone in the crowd caught a glimpse of her silhouette and the whispering began. The murmur crescendoed, then the audience erupted in frenzied applause. They clapped and cried with overwhelming emotion for the woman standing before them, for all she represented. She was a born-again Cinderella, a sanctified survivor. And if Rachel could do it, then they could, too; of this they were certain. Before them stood an exemplary woman devoted to her family and her calling, a faithful heroine in a faithless world. Not one of them doubted the power of love demonstrated by their beloved Rachel.

Faith clapped the loudest, the biggest believer of all. She was both grateful for and delighted by her status in Rachel's organization, an essential cog in the nonprofit machine, an indispensable member of the ministry family. Not that she needed another family. Her husband was a kind, gentle man, in contrast to her intensity. He quietly admired his wife's fervor and helped out when she was on the road with Rachel. In fact, that very morning, he delivered their three sons to the library for a homeschoolers' session. Faith preferred homeschooling for its multitasking efficiency. She could spend 30 minutes in the garden while the boys read; mix the bread and let it rise while she called out spelling words; throw in a load of laundry during their lunch break. Faith thrived under pressure like a plant under a sunlamp.

Faith mentally ran through her checklist as she parked her Volvo. *Good,* she thought. *It's all been covered.* She couldn't help but smile at her own competency. *Control is good*, she nodded to herself. *No disasters.*

Shelby's attention shifted from the dead woman to the blonde one getting out of the station wagon. Her heart pounded as each frame documented the progression of the assistant in the floral skirt and long rose-colored sweater, worn briefcase swinging in one hand, file folder in the other, Birkenstocks flapping against the soles of her feet. Shelby tapped the shutter at the precise moment Faith saw the naked body.

Oh, dear God, reacted Faith. *What is a naked woman doing here?* Shelby recorded Faith's dilemma as it twitched across her face: *For crying out loud, why hasn't* someone *moved her?* Faith rummaged in her bag for her cell phone, held it up in front of her eyes, hesitated, then slowly dropped it back in her bag. *I don't have time to call the police. I'll have to answer questions, fill out forms, make a statement . . . it will all take too much time. Someone inside needs to handle this.*

Faith wagged her head at the body indenting the mulch. *What kind of life leads a woman to this? I wonder if she's a prostitute or a gang member? I don't dare touch her; what if she has AIDS or is HIV positive?* Only then did Faith peer more closely at her dark hair and caramel skin. *I can't tell if she's Hispanic or Italian or what.* A leggy bug scurried up the woman's arm. Faith clamped her hand over her mouth and looked away. *If I had more time,* she thought, *I would take care of this. But my first responsibility is to take care of Rachel.* She glanced around the parking lot. *And Rachel is not here. I need to find her.*

Shelby snapped a final shot of Faith squeezing through Sissy's front door. Her camera and jaw fell in synchronized amazement. *What is going on? Is there something I can't see from here? Why aren't they helping her? I'm gonna go check it out.*

Inquisitiveness rather than concern made the reporter loop the camera strap around her neck. She reached for the door handle then hesitated when a third car drove up. Shelby lifted the Nikon, ever the observer behind the safety of her lens.

The Encounter

I count no human being a stranger.
—TERENCE, ROMAN POET, C. 190–159 B.C.

*Be not biased with compassion to the poor,
or favor to the rich, in point of justice.*
—SIR MATTHEW HALE, 1609–1676

Sammi was tired. *I'm getting too old for this,* she moaned to herself. The hot pink OPEN sign at Sissy's Country Kitchen was like a duck call to her faded old Honda. She shut off the shimmying engine. It was way past time for a tune-up, but that expense would just have to wait.

It's not like her job wasn't a good-paying gig. Even though the double-wide trailer she lived in was paid for, expenses were high. Her nephew's medical bills were mounting against minimal insurance coverage. Sammi had promised her dying sister that she would raise Dakota the best she could, not knowing he had inherited his mother's fatal disease.

Sammi pressed her fingertips to her eyelids. It had been years since Nikki died, but she still missed their all-night talks. Her most treasured memories involved her sister: talking in their made-up language, dancing at Nikki's wedding, holding Dakota seconds after he was born. Then the wrenching memories of wiping vomit off her sister's face, a cruel reaction to the chemotherapy and radiation. Combing and trimming Nikki's hair until every auburn strand had fallen out. Buying colorful silk scarves to cover her sister's baldness. And then burying her.

There was no time for self-pity, not with five-year-old Dakota depending on her. When Nikki died, Sammi tucked her college acceptance letter into a kitchen drawer, along with all her other adolescent dreams. They were replaced by a child's needs. More and more frequently she found herself tucking Dakota between the sheets of a hospital bed where he fought his own battle for life. She put away any hopes for a perfect job. For ready cash, she worked double shifts as a waitress. The promotion to bartender brought in fists full of tips, but she worked hard for every dollar. The next transition was a necessity; she needed more money. Sammi knew she was good at her job. But she hated her job description. She cringed at the word *stripper*. She much preferred the term *exotic dancer*.

Sammi went to work in the evenings, but carefully avoided any talk about what she did. All Dakota knew was that Aunty-Mom was beside his bed every morning when he woke up and stayed until she kissed him goodnight when his dinner tray arrived. She spent the day with him playing games, watching movies, working on school papers. When chemo exhausted him, she read stories of wizards and witches, princes and princesses, monsters under water and aliens on distant planets. If he was awake, she was there. Lately he noticed Aunty-Mom curled up on the fold-up cot next to his barred bed. With a child's sense of knowing, he kept quiet and let her sleep.

Every night before she left for work, Sammi and Dakota performed their ritual. Sammi pointed to a scrap of paper taped to the phone and said, "You need anything, you call me, you King of Needles," she said. "OK, you Queen of Wimps," he always answered.

Last night, drug-induced terrors woke him, and he dialed her number. On the fifth ring, she answered like she was thrilled to hear his voice. "What's up, Sir Needles?" she shouted over the loud music. When he asked where she was, she said that some people were celebrating a birthday. "Is it a fun party?" he asked. "More than you'll ever know," she teased. Just hearing her voice comforted him and he hung up, sleepy and warm.

Sammi was thinking about their conversation as she pulled into the parking lot of Sissy's. *Will he celebrate a twenty-first birthday? Go to college, laugh with friends, fall in love?* She really didn't want to know the answers. A chorus of sparrows circled overhead, dipping and climbing in their spontaneous concert. She wished she could sleep to their song. *Not an option,* she knew as she rubbed her eyes. But a good cup of coffee would be a nice treat before going to the hospital. Maybe even a Danish.

Shelby steadied the camera around her neck and got out of the car. She couldn't help but stare at Sammi's massive breasts bound by a black spandex halter. An oiled washboard stomach and a shapely behind rippled in shorts about as concealing as Saran Wrap. Shelby gawked at Sammi's wild mane of braids and beads.

Habit and instinct caused Shelby to lean against the fender and lift the camera to her eye. She centered on the graceful stride of the dancer and snapped several frames before Sammi blurted out, "Oh, Honey!" at first sight of the naked woman. *Didn't expect her to say that,* Shelby thought.

She crouched down in mirror motion with Sammi to capture the look of horror and heartbreak. Sammi heard the click and looked up.

"Stop taking pictures," she demanded. "Go get the two paper sacks out of my car!" Shelby jumped to obey as if ordered by her own mother. The camera bounced against her chest as she ran to the weather-worn hatchback. She jerked open the door and lifted out two bags. Glass bottles clinked against each other as Shelby ran back.

Sammi grabbed the bags out of Shelby's arms and dug through the contents. She pulled out a tall bottle, yanked out the cork with her teeth, then poured a trickle of white wine on each bloody gash.

Shelby started to protest. "She's crawling with bugs," Sammi calmly explained. "This will kill them or at least make them leave." Shelby leaned into the bushes and gagged.

"I need your help," Sammi said. It wasn't a request, but it wasn't harsh. Shelby wiped her mouth on her sleeve and turned back to Sammi. "Find the aloe in that bag," she instructed. Shelby did as she was told and handed Sammi a

half-filled bottle of green goo. Sammi spun off the cap,
poured out a glob, and warmed it in her hands. Then she
pressed her palms on the crusted sores. The woman moaned
in hazy consciousness, severely beaten but unbroken. *She's
not dead,* Shelby thought, with an uncharacteristic surge of
surprise.

Sammi carefully covered every jagged cut, gently mas-
saging the woman's arms and legs, her tender actions a word-
less song. Even Shelby was calmed by the silent melody. She
glanced over at Sammi and only then noticed the tears glis-
tening on painted cheeks.

Sammi lifted the battered woman's head and quietly
asked, "Honey, what's your name? Honey, wake up. You're
safe now, Honey. I've got you."

The woman's eyes rolled under swollen lids, a cry gurgled
behind split lips. "It's okay, Honey," Sammi assured her.
"What's your name?"

"Anya." Her slurred reply exposed broken teeth.

"Anya, is there anyone we can call; someone to come get
you?" Sammi asked. Anya shook her head no.

"Well, Anya, Honey, you're all right now. Don't worry
about a thing. I've got you and I'll take care of you." Sammi
struggled to lift Anya into her arms and motioned for Shelby
to open the glass doors.

Shelby held the two paper sacks and pressed herself
against the door frame as Sammi strode past, through the
diner, directly to the motel's registration desk. "Help!" Sammi
yelled. "Help! We need some help in here!" Shelby glanced
around the reception area, looking for someone, anyone, to
assist them. A greasy-haired manager exploded from a back
room, took one look, and started to shout. "Get that woman
out of here; we're a respectable business and we don't want
your kind in here."

"What kind is that," Sammi growled. "This woman needs
help, and she's gonna get it. Now give me a room so I can

get her fixed up." She twisted to look back at Shelby. "Go get my purse out from under the driver's seat."

Shelby ran, not wanting to miss a moment of action at the counter. She raced back with Sammi's turquoise, plastic beach bag.

Sammi and the manager were still glaring at each other. Sammi balanced the injured woman against the reception counter, then dug with one hand though her bag until she found three wadded up hundred-dollar bills. She flung them on the counter and rebalanced Anya.

The manager fixed his eyes on the money. His hand darted up and grabbed the cash the way a lizard's tongue nabs unsuspecting flies.

"She'll stay at least a week," Sammi said, "and if she needs to rest another week, I'll pay in advance. You make sure she gets three full meals a day. I'll be checking on her from time to time."

Shelby jerked the key out of the manager's hand, and dashed ahead to unlock the door. She propped it open with the paper bags, rushed to the bed, and pulled back the covers. Sammi gently lowered Anya on the clean, white sheets.

Sammi strategically covered the woman's nakedness with towels and placed warm, wet washcloths on the silent patient's wounds. Anya started to whimper, partly from pain, partly from relief, but mostly in gratitude. Sammi half-lifted the woman into her arms and rocked her like a child, whispering safety.

Shelby looked away in embarrassment. She was a useless intruder on this pieta-like scene. Taking a picture didn't even enter her mind. There was nothing for her to do, so she tiptoed toward the door.

"Thank you," Sammi whispered in her direction. Shelby's eyes burned with guilt. She had done nothing, really. Nothing at all. She wanted to thank Sammi but didn't know how or why. Instead she just nodded and slipped out the door.

Walking down the hall, she tried to grasp the significance of what she had just seen. Of the three women, she never would have guessed Sammi as the one to lift Anya out of the dirt. No, four women. Guilt shrouded her. She dropped her head in shame, knowing she was like Rachel and Faith, a spectator, detached and safe in the confines of her apathy.

Out in the glaring sunshine, Shelby looked at the entrance to the auditorium. It took very little time for her to decide not to attend Rev. Rachel's conference. There was no need. She had already seen and felt the power of love.

CHAPTER 1

The Parable of the Good Samaritan

At First Glance

Luke 10:25-37

Just then a lawyer stood up to test Jesus. "Teacher," he said, "what must I do to inherit eternal life?"

[Jesus] said to him, "What is written in the law? What do you read there?"

He answered, "You shall love the Lord your God with all your heart, and with all your soul, and with all your strength, and with all your mind; and your neighbor as yourself."

And [Jesus] said to him, "You have given the right answer; do this, and you will live."

But wanting to justify himself, [the lawyer] asked Jesus, "And who is my neighbor?"

Jesus replied, "A man was going down from Jerusalem to Jericho, and fell into the hands of robbers, who stripped him, beat him, and went away, leaving him half dead. Now by chance a priest was going down that road; and when he saw him, he passed by on the other side. So likewise a Levite, when he came to the place and saw him, passed by on the other side. But a Samaritan while traveling came near him; and when he saw him, he was moved with pity. He went to him and bandaged his wounds, having poured oil and wine on them. Then he put him on his own animal, brought him to an inn, and took care of him. The next day he took out two denarii, gave them to the innkeeper, and said, 'Take care of him; and when I come back, I will repay you whatever more you spend.'

"Which of these three, do you think, was a neighbor to the man who fell into the hands of the robbers?"

[The lawyer] said, "The one who showed him mercy."

Jesus said to him, "Go and do likewise."

A Closer Look

Here is an instance of a significant language shift over time. Two thousand years ago, to call someone a Samaritan was to sling a denigrating insult. Now, being called a "Good Samaritan" is a compliment, synonymous with humanitarianism.

In the twenty-first century, the word "neighbor" no longer describes a person living in close proximity. With phone, fax, Internet, and Concorde jumping boundaries of time and space, the entire world is next door. So, in our borderless global village, do we still need help defining a true neighbor? What would happen if we considered every human our neighbor, regardless of creed, education, or economic status? Considered every woman our neighbor whether dressed in a chador, kimono, sari, or T-shirt imprinted with a pierced and studded musician?

Jesus' story, recorded in Luke 10, was prompted by a Hebrew lawyer (a theologian or student of Scripture) who asked, "What must I do to inherit eternal life?" Jesus answered the question with a question, "What do you read in the Torah?"

This was not a defensive response or a hostile confrontation. Their exchange led the scholar to the correct answer, to the Shema, the essence of the entire Torah. *"You shall love the Lord your God with all your heart, and with all your soul, and with all your strength."* Jesus' disciples and the gathered crowd nodded in agreement; the liturgy from Deuteronomy 6:4-5 was recited every morning and evening before prayer. The astute lawyer added a clause, *'with all your mind,'* and a commandment from Leviticus, *'love your neighbor as yourself.'*[1]

Jesus enthusiastically responded to the inquirer's intellectual grasp and challenged him to live by his own words. "Great answer!" he said. "Now, go do that and you will live!" Jesus confirmed that love of God and neighbor is required, not as theory but as practice.

But that answer wasn't enough. The studious theologian pushed beyond the obvious and asked Jesus to define "neighbor." Was it with a sense of impatience? "Yeah, yeah, I *know* all that. But *who* is my neighbor?" Or was his conscience bothering him? Did he suspect that it took more than rote obedience to a set of rules and regulations to earn God's favor?

The lawyer probably did not expect Jesus to define "neighbor" with a parable set on the notorious seventeen-mile desert road between Jerusalem and Jericho. For a parable to be so specific in location was unusual, for like fairy tales, they were usually placed in fictional locations. But the hearers immediately visualized the very real and very dangerous road between "The Holy City" (nearly 2700 feet above sea-level) and "The City of Palm Trees" (820 feet below the Mediterranean by the Dead Sea). The connecting "Jericho Road"[2] dropped over 3500 feet,[3] twisting and turning through rocky terrain, providing excellent hiding places for bandits.[4]

To title this parable "The Good Samaritan" would have been as unacceptable as "The Kind Terrorist" would be to us today. Jews in Jesus' day never used *good* to define a Samaritan. Their mutual loathing, sustained for centuries, was the result of an enforced separation. Beginning in 722 B.C., waves of foreign invaders carried most of the Jewish population into captivity, leaving only a small remnant in Israel. Those left behind had intermarried with Gentiles. Worst of all, they no longer worshiped in Jerusalem, but had built their own temple. Jews who returned from exile rebuked, disassociated from, and hated the residents of Samaria, the "impure" Jews who had strayed from the traditions of the faith. The significant changes that occurred during their years of separation made reunification impossible. As propaganda is to truth, Samaritans were to Jews: close, but absolutely not the same.

Jesus deliberately chose his parable characters, knowing the story would rattle the listeners, just as his real-life interaction with Samaritans unsettled his disciples. Ignoring social and religious customs, he gave time and attention to a seemingly immoral Samaritan woman next to a well. To her, he first revealed that he was the Messiah. Chancing upon ten lepers on the road connecting Samaria and Galilee, Jesus was moved with compassion and healed them all. The only man to voice his thankfulness was a Samaritan, a fact Jesus pointedly brought to his disciples' attention. Jesus included a Samaritan in this parable to make most "evident that a good neighbor comes sometimes from the least expected quarter and that true charity transcends the limits of community."[5]

The story began with an injured traveler whom the listeners assumed to be Jewish. Was he? Without a stitch of clothing or piece of identification, no one could determine his tribe, village, or ethnic affiliation. What was he doing alone on a road known to be treacherous? For whatever reason, he was attacked, stripped, and abandoned by a group Jesus regularly criticized—thieves.[6]

Highway robbery set this parable in motion. A gang robbed a man, beat him unconscious, then fled, leaving him for dead. The lawyer and the surrounding audience waited for a hero's appearance. The Storyteller sensed their anticipation.

Jesus introduced a priest walking down the Jericho Road, not an unusual sight since twelve of Israel's twenty-four divisions of priests were based in Jericho. Each group looked forward to the annual privilege of serving two separate weeks in the temple. They usually journeyed together, but in this first scene of the story, a single cleric stumbled upon the apparently dead man.

Priests were highly educated, revered for their memorization of the Scriptures and study of the laws of Moses. What was this one thinking as he stood beside the battered body? Did he judge the value of the man left for dead? Assume the injured was a hooligan deserving of his fate? Shrug at what he assumed was a low-class citizen victimized by his own kind? Perhaps, perhaps not.

Perhaps the priest was preoccupied with his responsibilities, his prior commitments. Maybe he was rushing back to perform a wedding or circumcision. Maybe elders were waiting for him to fulfill some mandatory duty that he considered more important than helping an unworthy stranger. Properly made sacrifices, meticulously burned incense, and correct adherence to the liturgy met the letter of the religious law, which protected him from uncleanness. He couldn't risk defilement by impulsively giving help.

The priest was also confronted with the dilemma of obeying the letter of the *written* law or invoking the leniency of the *oral* law. Strict written law forbid him to touch a corpse; to do so would result in a week-long ritual of purification, rendering him useless in the activities of the temple. He couldn't afford to lose seven precious days in isolation. But that's not reason enough to let him off the hook. According to *oral* law, if a priest found a neglected corpse on the road, he could touch the body without threat of uncleanness. If no other person was available to bury the deceased, burial took priority over religious purity, no matter how inconvenient.

The priest stood in the middle of the road and considered his options. In a moment of decisiveness, rigid legalism propelled him forward. He left the man lying in the ditch.

So much for the priest as the hero. What was the lawyer thinking at this point in the story? What were the disciples thinking? Should or shouldn't this representative of God have helped the victim? Was there a clearly right thing to do? Was this an occasion of situational ethics? This wasn't easy.

The crowd around Jesus stood in silence, waiting for someone else to come to the rescue. So, the Storyteller introduced the next character.

A Levite appeared on the road, a temple assistant whose work was to accept the tithes and to prepare the sacrificial animals and grains. He stopped and stared at the unrecognizable victim. Like the priest, he, too, considered seven lost days imposed by touching a corpse.

In his work, and in this drama, the Levite followed the priest's lead. Did he know that the priest was just ahead of him? If so, he correctly surmised from the telltale footprints that his esteemed leader stopped, assessed the situation, and moved on. Would the Levite devotedly follow a priestly example?

If the priest's actions were unknown to him, what was the Levite thinking? Maybe he feared the fallen man was a decoy, a robber acting injured so an unsuspecting traveler would stop, allowing hidden accomplices to jump out and attack. Maybe he concluded that being alone on this road was an invitation for violence. Perhaps he was afraid to touch the body, nauseated by the sight of bloody flesh. As a common man, a lay-associate in the synagogue, maybe he categorized the victim as one of "them," certainly not one of "us."

For whatever reason, the Levite, like the priest, showed no emotional response: no pity, no quest for justice, no mourning. If he felt it, he did not act on it. He gathered up his proud cloak of excuses and continued on his journey, leaving the victim sprawled in the dirt.

It is important to notice two things here. One, both travelers were walking *down* from Jerusalem to Jericho. They had already fulfilled their obligations in the temple, so a week of purification would not have deferred their service. Two, the man brutally robbed was not described as dead; he was half-dead, beaten so severely he hung between life and death. So, these men were not excused from giving care since oral tradition *required* the preservation of life at all costs. These men were more concerned with their own purity than with saving the life of another man.

What was the lawyer thinking by the end of the second scene? How was the crowd reacting to the story? Did they offer understanding to these two distinguished members of the faith, justifying their behavior because of their position, their social prominence? Or did Jesus' insinuation that religious leaders were not necessarily pious but elitist cause hair to bristle on the back of some necks? Did they see through his thinly veiled reference to the tension between Jewish peasants and the temple aristocracy? Did some hearers nod their heads in agreement, convinced that these first two characters were unconcerned with the plight of rural Jews?

The crowd shuffled, anticipating a third character, a good Israelite, to come to the rescue. In scene three, Jesus introduced the hero by saying, "A Samaritan traveling by..." Listeners were shocked. A hostile murmur nearly drowned out the rest of the story. *A Samaritan? He's no hero, he's a villain!* In melodramatic response, men laughed with contempt, the devout turned their backs in disgust, horrified clergy covered their mouths with their hands. *A Samaritan? No way. Not a scum, not a moral deviant. Jews don't do business with Samaritans, so what was he doing on this road from Jerusalem anyway?* Seething listeners glared at the Storyteller. Who did this carpenter, this self-appointed teacher, think he was, elevating and exemplifying a Samaritan? He was telling it wrong. The rescuer should be a Jewish layperson, a Roman soldier, even a repentant robber, but *never* a Samaritan.

Their reaction was typical. Jews "cursed the Samaritans publicly in the synagogues, and prayed to God that they should have no share in eternal life; they would not believe the testimony of a Samaritan nor accept a service from one."[7] Their "separation was not only something religious, but was seen as important in preserving the Jewish national and cultural identity in a threatening time of political and cultural imperialism."[8]

Were Samaritans deserving of such hatred in light of their Jewish heritage? They worshiped YAHWEH and adhered to the teachings of the Torah, the five books of Moses. They, too, were forbidden to touch a corpse. And they reciprocally detested the Jews. But this idealized Samaritan's compassion superseded his obedience to the law. Even though he understood the risk of ritual defilement, he risked much more: He could be attacked by hidden robbers or be accused of the crime. Still, he stopped to help.

The audience fumed, knowing full well that a parable was a fictional story portraying truth. They knew they were to choose the character that best represented themselves. That, however, was impossible in this case. They were expecting the triad of a priest, Levite, and Israelite—but the Storyteller eliminated the Israelite by inserting a heretical foreigner. The priest and Levite passed by, leaving listeners with a choice between the half-dead man in the care of the despised Samaritan (which was not really an option) or an adamant denial that the parable reflected their world. The hearer who expected a heroic Israelite to come along finds that the only hero is a Samaritan.[9]

The furious crowd had heard only the half of it. For those who remained listening, Jesus described a merciful Samaritan who tenderly poured wine and oil on the victim's wounds and then bound them with strips of his own garments. "Blasphemy!" they cried. The symbolism of purifying wounds with oil and wine, holy elements of sacrifice offered by the priest and the Levite in the temple, was not lost on them. They knew God as the one who "binds up their wounds."[10] Now, Jesus purposefully compared the compassion of the Samaritan to the mercy of God. Unimaginable! And it was only going to get worse.

The Samaritan carried the unconscious man to an inn[11] and tended to him throughout the night. The next morning, he prepaid for the victim's convalescence with two denarii, the equivalent of two days wages for a common laborer, enough to cover the cost of twenty-four nights at an inn. "A person with an unpaid debt could be enslaved until the debt was paid. Since the injured man was robbed and stripped—deprived of all resources—he could have been at the mercy of the innkeeper, a profession that had a reputation in antiquity for dishonesty and violence. The Samaritan assures the injured man's freedom and independence."[12]

He did more than just rescue the victim; he directly affected his future. When the Samaritan told the innkeeper that he would return, it was not only to settle the final bill, but to make sure the patient received the care that was purchased and that no additional harm was inflicted. The crowd openly scoffed at the absurdity of such behavior.

With perhaps a hint of cunning, Jesus asked a final question. "So, which of these three, *do you think*, was a neighbor to the man who fell into the hands of the robbers?" What a remarkable question that reverberates in our ears 2000 years later. *What do you think?*

The lawyer's earlier recitation of the Shema added the decree that one should love God "with your mind." Now, at the end of the parable, Jesus held him to it. "Since you added 'mind,' here is an opportunity for you to use it. *What do you think?*" Between the lines of the story, Jesus asked people to *think*, to ponder mercy, to consider change, to balance righteousness against tradition. Then he asked the lawyer to see the possibility of relationships from God's perspective. The parable was a reflection of both what is and what can be.

Conflict was implicit in the lawyer's second question and in the answer given by Jesus. The lawyer looked outward and asked, "Who is my neighbor?" Jesus wanted him to look inward and ask, "How am I to live as a neighbor?" The lawyer determined the worthiness of others; Jesus asserted that compassion is not dependent on a recipient's qualifications or worthiness. There were no qualifiers in Jesus' command: "Love your enemies, do good to those who hate you, bless those who curse you, pray for those who abuse you."[13] This parable personalizes Jesus' Sermon on the Mount: "You have heard that it was said, 'You shall love your neighbor and hate your enemy.' But I say to you, 'Love your enemies.' "[14]

A critical shift occurred when Jesus asked, "Who proved to be the neighbor?" The focus moved "from the person to whom care is shown onto the person who is showing care."[15] I wonder if the lawyer's reply was tinged with derision as he correctly identified a neighbor as "The one who showed him mercy." Interestingly, he did not say the loathsome word "Samaritan."

Perhaps the lawyer replied with a tone of sincere understanding. Maybe he looked Jesus in the eye and acknowledged the startling truth of the parable: The one who showed mercy was a model of inclusiveness. The Samaritan was no longer identified by his heritage or cultural community but by his compassion. The lawyer acknowledged the dissolution of boundaries between insiders and outsiders, the clean and the unclean, the haves and have-nots. After hearing one simple story from Jesus, lines of distinction were erased and the neighborly circle expanded to include anyone in need.

Again, Jesus approvingly smiled at the lawyer's wisdom and said, "Go and do likewise." The original question, "What must I do?" had been answered. It's one thing to *know* what to do; it's quite another to *do* it.

Throughout his adult life, Jesus inhabited his own parables: he taught, healed the sick, and fed the hungry out of his compassion.[16] As the very incarnation of God, he associated with and showed concern for sinners, tax collectors, widows, cripples, the poor, the blind and maimed, the very individuals shunned by the very religious. God, as portrayed by his Son, values all the children on earth and requires that we treat one another with merciful care. God's children are not to live as enemies, only neighbors.

CHAPTER 2

Looking Beyond Reputation

❧

Behind the Image

I found it difficult to choose modern women to represent the men in the parable. Ordained women in the pulpit aren't exactly common, and many denominations still close the eldership and deaconate to women. Who in our enlightened society is equal to a Samaritan, so resolutely despised by religious people? Who would you choose?

Shelby, a spectator of Rachel, Faith, and Sammi, represents those who watch us: neighbors, coworkers, relatives, spouses, children, and friends. We often bustle through life, unaware of their silent scrutiny. Every gesture we make, attitude we project, each action directed toward others gets measured against our professions of faith. Who is your Shelby?

The reporter was critical of Rachel's apparent lack of compassion, her aversion to get involved. As headlines frequently indicate, clergy are not exempt from sin, wrong choices, or failures. Some of us who "idolize" Christian celebrities have been guilty of pushing pedestals under them in a desire to associate with their specialness. Then, when those we elevate turn out to be flawed humans, our adoration turns to condemnation, our criticism grows loud, our punishment becomes disassociation or even expulsion. I wonder if Shelby wrote an article about Rachel. Did she print the photographs she had taken? Did she tell her editor the truth? Is Shelby's perspective of the truth different from Rachel's?

Rachel—The Priest

Rachel was committed to her calling, obedient to doing "the Lord's work." Like many clerics, she tried to define the limits and boundaries of her vocation. A work-outside-the-home wife and mother, she struggled against the myth of doing and having it all. She realized there aren't enough hours in a day to give attention to marriage, motherhood, career, running a household, participating in church, volunteering in the community...not to mention the necessary pleasures of reading, playing, and stopping to smell the daisies.

Rachel measured success by the number of women applauding in the audience. The effectiveness of her ministry was based on the per-person dollar average of product sales. Relevance was determined by the amount of television, radio, and public appearances on her calendar. Her story raises the question of how success is rightly measured. When is it *actually* achieved?

Estrangement from her family and absence from her congregation were the exchange Rachel made for public adoration and national fame. A simple willingness to give her testimony had evolved into a complex machine that required constant attention. Her personal life, time with her husband and children, and worship with her own church were governed by the obligations of her work. Are these consequences of overscheduling or unavoidable sacrifice? Can obedience to God lead to a confusion of priorities, or is this something created by seeking success?

Rachel's compassion was reserved for those who registered for her conferences, worked on her staff, or attended her church. Her concern weakened as it extended out. Like Rachel, many of us are unaware that we calculate the worthiness of a person before offering our help. If they're one of "us," we are quick to lend a helping hand. If they're one of "them," our hands remain clenched in our pockets.

Perhaps Rachel believed her "calling" was to a select few. Many clergy or parachurch organizations focus on specific issues, demographics, or interests. And that can be a good thing. Rachel's calling is not under question; she, like the priest, had a job to do and, in all likelihood, did it well. But her encounter with Anya was special, beyond the limits of her job. This *personal* encounter was an opportunity not to develop her compassion, but to reveal it. Some of us are almost professional Christians, doing the right thing, the expected thing, within the confines of our faith environment. Do we behave or react differently in a secular or unfamiliar setting?

Rachel condemned the woman in the dirt, forgetful of her own previous stint in the mire. Like her, we often believe our own failings merit a generous measure of grace. It's different when it happens to us, a debacle when it happens to them.

This parable is usually cast as an example for doing good works, a lesson for going outside our comfort zone or helping those less fortunate than ourselves. I believe, however, that Jesus shifts our attention from what we must *do* to *who we are*. Jesus expects us to be, without reservation, loving neighbors.

Faith—The Levite

Faith's identity and worth were interwoven with Rachel's. Whatever Rachel did, Faith did, a mimicking shadow of a powerful presence. She shielded Rachel and herself from the realities of the outside world. Then, when confronted by a situation where a specific woman was in desperate need, she justified her uninvolvement by lack of time, by her duty to those waiting for her to make a good thing happen.

Schedule governed Faith's every move. She made no allowance for emergencies; she did only what "should" be done, what she found neatly printed on today's "Things to Do" list. Her devotion to the women attending Rachel's conferences was admirable, but her neglect of those outside the auditorium was not. A literal or figurative fear of touching domestic violence or AIDS in no way exempted Faith from Jesus' command to clothe the naked, feed the hungry, heal the sick, and care for the widows and orphans. Care for "our own" can never exempt us from caring for others.

Faith believed, like many women, that control can eliminate disaster or conflict. If only that were true. Rarely can life be held under control. Unexpected events and people are the color of life. This parable shows us that when an opportunity for mercy arises, avoidance is not an acceptable option. God expects us to get our hands dirty, to adjust our perfect plans, and to take a risk for the sake of others.

It is not easy for intelligent, organized women to be inconvenienced, even for God's sake. Women like Faith wear titles of "executive assistant" or "corporate scheduler." (I know—I was one for many years.) These are powerful, efficient, no-nonsense roles. "Neighbor," however, is a blurry word. Neighbors stop to visit, they borrow, they interrupt routine. Faith tolerated neighbors when they came to her; she never had a need to go to them. Radiant in her self-sufficiency, Faith represents those of us who may well care but only on our own terms and timetable.

Pride is not one of the fruits of the Spirit, and Faith would have denied that she was proud of her accomplishments. But, after all, who could deny that her efficient office, Rachel's success, three obedient children, and a spotless home were the results of proficiency and perfectionism. She believed control of her children's education would prevent unwelcome influences in their lives, would keep them safe from drugs, weapons, and peer pressure. Faith, who understood the meaning of compassion, who taught the "service" Scriptures to her children, who worked in a Christian organization with a pious mission statement, failed to integrate knowledge with actions outside the confines of her safe environment. In an unscheduled moment, she could not, or did not, think more highly of others than herself.

Sammi—The Samaritan

I struggled over giving Sammi an occupation. She needed to be a woman easily discarded or at least discounted by "decent" people. Does any one ethnic group or profession or religious faction currently bear the hatred and contempt ancient Jews felt for Samaritans? In the history of the United States, a variety of racial hatreds induced ridicule, repression, ostracization, even violence. Later, these same hostilities were aimed at people suspected of being Communists; then to those suffering from AIDS, to homosexuals, to illegal aliens. Who will be the next victims of discrimination, whether racial, intellectual, religious, or nationalistic? In truth, in the modern world we cannot choose our neighbor. Rather, we are commanded to be a neighbor. Sammi is the example Jesus chose to shame religious pride.

The cost exacted by compassion can be high. Sammi paid hard-earned cash for Anya's convalescence, money originally budgeted for her nephew's treatment. Her schedule was thrown off, her journey interrupted. She endured criticism when compassion caused her to touch a situation considered "untouchable."

To fully plumb the parable's meaning, we must ask *why* Sammi exhibited such great compassion. Had she helped the battered, the robbed, the abandoned before? Had she seen the hurt, the disenfranchised, the outcast in her own house or maybe in her own mirror? Sammi knew what it felt like to be neither socially or economically powerful. She knew what it was like to live without—without luxuries, without safety, without sufficient medical insurance, without respect. She knew what it meant to be leered at, to be demeaned. Because she knew, she identified with Anya. She treated a stranger as she wished to be treated. She, of all people, embodied the Golden Rule.

In this parable, a consistent pattern is formed by the actions of the three characters: they see, they react. Rachel and Faith see and pass by. Sammi sees and stops. "Compassion is the bridge between simply looking on injured and half-dead fellow human beings and entering their world with saving care. Compassion is that divine quality which, when present in human beings, enables them to share deeply in the sufferings and needs of others."[1]

Jesus widened the boundaries of God's people to include those we are inclined to exclude. Jesus' choice of a Samaritan, seemingly a religious apostate, challenges our understanding of God. "The graciousness of God often comes from those least expected, from the outcast. It often comes amid powerlessness. It challenges us to move beyond our social and religious constructs of good and evil; it subverts our tendency to divide the world into insiders and outsiders. It makes us realize that goodness may be found precisely in those we often call evil or enemy."[2]

Sammi is an admirable woman, not just because she did the right thing at the right time. Sammi is admirable because she gave what she had, her oil and wine, her time and money, to tend the wounds of a suffering representation of Christ. Anya, not Sammi, is the Christ-figure in this parable. Jesus aligned himself with the lowly when he said in Matthew 25:34-36: "I was hungry and you gave me food, I was thirsty and you gave me something to drink, I was a stranger and you welcomed me, I was naked and you gave me clothing, I was sick and you took care of me, I was in prison and you visited me. Truly I tell you, just as you did it to one of the least of these who are members of my family, you did it to me."

Often, we do not recognize Christ in the form of the destitute, the battered, the weak, just as many in the crowd hearing his parable failed to recognize him in the form of the Messiah. They were blinded by his association with outcasts, his compassion for the unclean. They could not see the image of God behind his silence at his trial, in the torn flesh from his beating, beyond his nakedness on the cross; not in his agony between two thieves, his burial in the tomb of death. They did not see him in his resurrection.

This parable is not only about good works. It is not only about the Samaritan's deeds. I believe it is about seeing and responding to Christ, his woundedness, his hunger and his pain, in the bodies of the suffering; in the millions of civilians around the world displaced by war; in Africans dying from famine; the homeless under American bridges; the drug addicts in good homes; the molested, malnourished, illiterate children abandoned in our global village. When we imitate the Samaritan, we are a part of the "mystery of redemption."[3] When we stop our daily routine to care for Christ in an unrecognizable guise, we can be called a "Good Samaritan."

Seeing Ourselves

An "us vs. them" environment, reminiscent of centuries of animosity between Jews and Samaritans, still exists between some American Christians and their culture, between the "saved" and the "secular." My husband and I recently rented a video, a comedic spoof on Hollywood stars and filmmakers. In one scene, a mother and father plead with their runaway teenager to return home. In opposition, his band of friends shout at him to stay, then turn to deride the parents. The final screamed expletive in the tirade was, "You *Christians!*" I winced. Why, out of all the words in the English language, was that one chosen to describe parents concerned with their son's choices? Do Christians deserve such hostility? Is the label "Christian" an expletive earned by our actions, our attitudes?

Did the Samaritans deserve the loathing of the Jews? True, during a Passover between C.E. 6 and 9, they scattered human bones throughout the Jerusalem Temple court. This was a justifiable defilement, in their opinion, because Jews had destroyed their own temple over a hundred years earlier. The Jews rationalized their hatred of the Samaritans with words like "impure" and "mixed race." The rubble of Bosnia is proof that neighbors still destroy one another's property based on ethnic or religious retribution. The Protestant/Catholic hostility in Ireland is a continuation of events that began centuries ago. Here in the United States, September 11 will be a reminder of how thoroughly brutal battles of ideology can be. How did we respond to "them"? Are we willing to use our 4-wheel-drive SUV to pull a Muslim out of a ditch? Offer money to a stranded Buddhist monk? We don't immediately get involved, we don't associate with "them" because our motives may be misinterpreted or because we oppose their success. When will the slinging of insults end? Who will take the first step to eliminate separation among those who pledge allegiance to Christ? Who models the example of the Samaritan, a living reflection of compassion in our family, our neighborhood, our world?

There is no denying that caring for the needy is personally costly. We Americans, particularly, have little tolerance for inconvenience. It is enough to be distracted by the needs of friends. If we are honest, tending to the needs of strangers, aside from contributing to charities and churches, stretches us to the point of impatience. Would we consider arriving at our destination a day late in order to spend the night in a motel or hospital tending to the needs of a stranger?

The original hearers of this parable were hard-pressed to choose a character with whom they could identify. Which character strikes a familiar chord with us? Do we resemble the priestly Rachel, distracted by our own religious agenda, impressed with our sanitized importance? Secure in our middle- to upper-level income group, sequestered from the lower classes? Have we become professional Christians who quote Scripture to prove or placate our own point of view?

Are we represented by the Levitical Faith, so busy in our well-ordered service that no time exists for those outside the daily plan? Are we driven by the pursuit of perfection rather than excellence? Are we proud of our orderly, confined world?

Then there's Sammi: Sammi who is good but embarrassing to us. How can we possibly relate to a woman like her? To what extreme would we go if we had to earn money to save a dying child? How do we feel when an "outsider" acts Christ-like?

All three characters faced the same opportunity when they saw Anya. Rachel and Faith avoided her, Sammi knelt to help her. On our new millennium journey, how do we respond to victims littering the road: the sufferers of oppression and mental illness; those battered by spousal abuse, drug addiction, financial ruin? Are we stopped in our tracks by overwhelming compassion? Would Jesus use your name, my name, as a model of a good neighbor?

We have fully examined the three main characters of the story. But there is one more: Anya. Without Anya, there is no need for Sammi. There are no details about Anya's age, race, education, ethnic origin, religion, political affiliation, or food preferences. But I wonder where she was going, what she was doing, why she was alone, and how she survived such a brutal attack.

In truth, Anya cannot be identified. She is a composite drawing of us. We are the wounded woman. We are beaten down by disappointments, responsibilities, depression. We are robbed of our childhood dreams, from achieving our goals, of a chance to be equal. Our futures are stolen by breast cancer, Alzheimer's, pink slips, unfairness. We are abandoned by family, society, by those we expected to love us.

We are bruised by life's harsh realities; we are naked in our distress. We need a hand of mercy to lift us from the road and carry us to clean sheets of hope. We are desperate for healing conclusions to our stories.

In Jesus' call to neighborliness, we see ourselves. Often, we are as callous and haughty as Rachel, as judgmental as Faith. In this parable, Jesus implores us to be as compassionate as Sammi. And should we find ourselves lying in a ditch called divorce, abandonment, or widowhood; in a pile of dirt marked failure, disaster, or inferiority; in a gravel pit named despair, fear, or hopelessness, we pray for a Good Samaritan to stop. We may be surprised by who shows up.

CHAPTER 3

Reflections of Neighborliness

🌿

I was both surprised and pleased one day when Zoe unexpectedly arrived at my house for a visit. We met only a few weeks earlier when I attended my first neighborhood Bunko party (a *whole* other story). Zoe was a spunky, fun-loving competitor, and I immediately liked her wit and sense of humor. *We could be friends,* I thought, after spending one evening with her.

I invited Zoe in, and on our way to the kitchen, she stopped in her tracks to stare at a modern crucifix hanging on our family room wall. The painting is an impressive 7½ feet tall by 2½ feet wide. A small woolly lamb in the bottom right corner gazes up at a Picasso-like Christ of ochre and cubed flesh against a deep blue storm of strokes, his body pierced by green wooden rods.

"Is that Jesus?" she asked.

"Yes," I replied.

"He was Jewish, right?"

"Yes."

"Well," Zoe said brightly, "so am I, so we have something in common. We both have paintings of Jews in our family rooms."

We laughed easily, but later I was struck by how hard she looked for something we held in common, as if to validate our budding friendship against our differing religious traditions. It wasn't enough for us to be residential neighbors; we each hoped for a neighborliness beyond dice games and party conversations.

Barbara Roberts Pine, in her own writings, tells of learning what it means to be a real neighbor. As a young wife of an Air Force fighter pilot, Barb lived in base housing on the island of Okinawa. Her home and that of her neighbor's faced each other across a small lawn, a postage stamp of grass Barb and Jan frequently ran across to borrow garlic, to chat, to play bridge, or to catch up on the latest rumors of military moves. It was a place to plant flowers and enjoy coffee, a place to while away time during their husbands' prolonged absences.

Marriage to pilots, residency in a foreign country, adjustments to a military environment were common topics, but not everything was similar for the two young women. Barb was a 22-year-old Conservative Baptist girl from the Southwest. Jan was a 25-year-old Catholic girl from the East. Barb was a mom. In her three years on that small island, she conceived, delivered and nurtured two baby boys. Jan, too, easily conceived, even frequently, but each pregnancy ended in miscarriage. She remained childless. However, her current pregnancy was going well.

One summer day, a typhoon threatened the serenity and security of the island. As was the routine in such circumstances, military pilots and planes were safely dispatched to Japan. As usual, pilot wives were left behind to batten down the hatches, which literally meant boarding up windows, stowing lawn chairs, children's toys, and any potentially flying objects, and stocking up on supplies. A party atmosphere grew as women ran from the BX to the commissary in high winds and warm rains, filling shopping carts with diapers, bottled water, baby food, Sterno, batteries, and candles. When the storm hit, they would be snug, prepared, and relatively safe.

Barb was home, searching for candlesticks when, for her, the party ended. Jan's stricken voice rose above the wind.

The terrified tone of her cry caused Barb to scramble off a stepstool and sprint across their shared lawn. She barged into Jan's living room in time to see her neighbor stumble from the bathroom to her bedroom, strands of strawberry blonde hair stuck to her sweaty face, pale, and frightened.

"I need to go to the hospital," Jan said. "But first, I need you to baptize my baby." A wave of nausea rolled through Barb, a sickening knowledge that for the fifth time, in the fifth month of pregnancy, Jan had miscarried. "No, no!" Barb silently cried. No—to yet another lost infant. No—to Jan's last request. As thoroughly as Barb was Baptist, Jan was Catholic, a woman of devout faith who tended to first things first. And at this moment, Jan was convinced that she had a limited time to rescue her baby from Limbo, a doctrine Barb denied.

Jan fell onto her bed, weeping, bleeding, quivering in shock. Barb, in her own form of shock, picked up a phone from the nightstand and dialed the chapel. The priest immediately grasped the urgency of the situation and promptly questioned Barb's theology. "Do you believe in the holy trinity?" he asked. Barb bristled. She was a *Baptist* for heaven's sake. She wanted to shout, "Who better than Baptists believe in the trinity?" She politely replied, "I do." In retrospect, she realized that he was as concerned about her beliefs as she was about his. After receiving instructions, Barb hung up the phone. She quickly moved to the bathroom, immersed her hands into the toilet pool of dark and fresh blood and lifted out a small, soft mass. Trembling, she cupped water from the faucet into one hand and poured it in the sign of the cross over the lifeless form. Loudly enough for its mother to hear, Barb said, "In the name of the Father, of the Son, and of the Holy Spirit, I baptize you, beloved child of Jan."

I often think about that exchange between my friend and her friend. Barb could have said, "Jan, relax, calm down, take a deep breath. Don't worry about the eternal security of your child. Your Church tradition, not the Bible, calls for this baptism." But those *words* would not have helped, would not have aided a hemorrhaging soul. Barb's *actions* spoke healing to a broken heart.

Barb deliberately set aside her strong beliefs about life and death, set aside her fears, her opinion. Jan didn't need Barb's theology or opinion. She needed compassion. She needed to be served, not straightened out. Barb, by her act of baptism that day, became a neighbor. A Good Samaritan kind of neighbor. She did not avoid conflict by crossing to the other side of the street. She gave herself to a personally uncomfortable situation for someone else's sake.

We walk on morally, theologically, and relationally dangerous roads today. I wonder if we don't make things worse, we who for denominational or sanctimonious reasons refuse to stop for the sake of others along our life's journey. We swagger along in elite cliques, unaware that the rest of the world watches with pained or puzzled expressions. We justify stepping over lifeless bodies, maimed by grief, stripped of dignity, robbed of hope, ignored by a community that chatters piety and good works. How different our world would be if we lived like the Good Samaritan, if our lives were governed by a heart of love rather than a doctrine of law.

The Image
of Forgiveness

Justine: A Fair Banker

❦

The First Meeting

The human species, according to the best theory I can form
of it, is composed of two distinct races,
the men who borrow, and the men who lend.
—CHARLES LAMB, 1775–1834

We find it as difficult to forgive a person for displaying his
feeling in all its nakedness as we do to forgive
a man for being penniless.
—HONORÉ DE BALZAC, 1799–1850

*G*abriella!" The young assistant was surprised by the severity of her boss's voice vibrating out of the intercom. She grabbed a pen and notepad, sprung from her ergonomic chair, and rushed into the elegant domain of her employer. She hurried across the plush carpet, her eyes locked on the President of Life Trust Bank.

Justine Brooke stood behind her massive cherry desk, arms stiff, fingers splayed over two thick stacks of papers. Her neck curved down, a curtain of blonde hair hiding her expression. *She has the stance of an angry bull,* Gabrie thought, *head lowered for a charge.* The palpable silence confirmed that someone was in trouble.

Justine lifted her head, eyes sparking. "Have Elena Holt in my office within the hour." Her words were as heated as a pressurized release of steam.

Gabrie nodded and backed toward the doors. With one hand on the brass handle, she hesitated for any additional instruction. There was none; Justine had made herself clear. Gabrie slipped out and hurried to her phone.

After one ring, Misty answered. "Elena Holt's office; Misty speaking."

"Hi, Misty, it's Gabriella at Life Trust. Ms. Brooke needs some time with Ms. Holt. Does she have any openings today?"

Misty was a new employee and her inexperience in the finer points of the verbal dance was immediately obvious. She should have replied, "Ms. Holt's tied up for the rest of the day and into the evening," then asked why the caller inquired. If the reason seemed important, an opening would have miraculously appeared. "Well, I can squeeze you in between 3:30 and 4:00." Top level executives aren't the only ones to play power games. Misty didn't know the rules and naively told the truth. "She's wide open all afternoon. How much time does Ms. Brooke need?"

The muffled sound coming through the receiver indicated that Elena was now standing by Misty's desk, emphatically signaling that she did not want to meet with Justine. The subsequent silence confirmed Misty's panic; she had already said that Elena was available, Elena was saying she wasn't.

Gabrie stifled a laugh. "Misty, are you there?"

"Uuhhhh…" warbled Misty. Gabrie ignored it. "Tell Ms. Holt our driver is on his way to pick her up. Kevin should be there in about ten minutes and I'll inform Ms. Brooke that Ms. Holt is on her way. Thanks, Misty." Gabrie quickly depressed the phone's receiver button, amused by Misty's failure to ask what the meeting was about. She had her own suspicion; seldom was a summons from her boss for social reasons. Only Justine knew the urgent reasons for Elena's appearance.

Gabrie released her finger for a dial tone then punched in Kevin's extension. When he answered, she filled him in on the details of his next run. "Better take Brian with you," she laughed. No one wanted to be alone with Elena, the self-proclaimed authority on acquisitions and stock-split investments and get-rich-quick schemes.

Less than half an hour later, Elena flounced from the elevator, followed by Kevin and Brian. Gabrie saw by the stricken looks on the men's faces that it had been quite a smelly journey. Instead of lightly dabbing her expensive perfume, Elena saturated herself in *Diamond Roses*. Hours after she left a place, the pervasive fragrance lingered as throat-burning evidence of her presence. Gabrie could only imagine how nauseating the car ride must have been. She threw an apologetic look at the drivers and stood.

"Welcome, Ms. Holt. Come right in. I'll bring you a Pelligrino. Would you like anything else?" Gabrie guided Elena into Justine's office. She looked to Justine, who was rising from her chair, and asked, "May I bring you something?" Justine nodded, her gaze fixed on Elena. The meeting was about to begin.

Neither woman noticed Gabrie's leaving. The tension between the two was as inescapable as Elena's perfume. Justine extended her hand to greet the woman she considered a conniver and a braggart. She despised Elena's blatant name-dropping and obsessive association with the rich, her need to join their elite clubs, eat in the same exclusive restaurants, ski on the same slopes. But in relation to Justine, Elena was not the same. Justine was a lender, Elena was a borrower.

Elena moved to the window in defiance of Justine's authority over her. "I love this view," she bubbled. "I'm glad you caught me when you called; my schedule is crammed today. Can't waste a second, you know. Time is money!"

Silence settled in the room. Elena turned to see Justine quietly sitting in her massive chair. So, no social chit-chat. This was all business. Elena chose one of the two small chairs in front of Justine's desk and lowered herself into the soft leather. "It's been so humid lately," she said, stalling Justine's purpose. "Have you taken a vacation yet? Robert and I had the *best* time on our Mediterranean cruise. The weather was perfect, the food was fabulous, and we met the most *gorgeous* Greeks and Italians!"

Justine considered both Elena's performance and her yellow silk suit hideous. *Only Elena would wear such a gaudy color,* she thought. Not a soft, buttery pastel, but a fierce, garish goldenrod, a comical palette with Elena's unnaturally red hair and crescents of iridescent blue eye shadow. She deliberately interrupted Elena's patter. "I've just reviewed your latest profit and loss statement."

Not a muscle moved in Elena's face. It was as if she hadn't heard Justine. Without much of a pause, she responded, "Must we talk here? Let's do a late lunch at that new sushi place; my treat." She started to rise.

Justine pointed to the papers on the desk. "I was bothered by some discrepancies."

Elena settled back into the chair and raised an eyebrow in feigned interest. Her visible animosity prompted Justine to get to the point.

"As you well know, the economy is not improving. The stock market took another plunge today. Even with the lowered interest rate, we're sliding into a recession. It's my job, my duty, to protect the bank."

Elena's heart lurched. Sweat surged like a menopausal hot flash. She grabbed the arms of the chair with the sensation of plummeting in an elevator. She knew, she knew without a doubt, what was coming. Justine was calling in her loans.

An involuntary moan escaped from her constricting throat. Muscles around her mouth ticked in spasmodic jerks. Justine pushed the intercom. "Gabriella, our water, please."

Gabrie carried in a silver tray, loaded with an ice-filled bucket, a pair of sterling tongs, a plate of sliced limes, and linen napkins. After setting the tray on the edge of the desk, she opened the green bottle, releasing a gassy mist. Elena grabbed for a glass, nearly knocking it over. Gabrie steadied the crystal, poured water over ice, and kept her eyes on her task. She handed the second glass to Justine. Without a word, she exited the office, plopped into her chair, picked up the phone and punched Kevin's number.

"You're not going to believe what's going on," she whispered to the man she was secretly dating. "Justine's calling in Elena's loans, and Elena seems about ready to faint. How I'd love to sit in on that meeting!" The two employees imagined the conversation between the two executives and speculated how Elena would try to finagle her way out of trouble.

Behind closed doors, Justine continued. "I was quite willing to take risks with you, Elena, often against my better judgment. I authorized funds for some 'iffy' investments. Some paid off well. Some didn't. That was the risk we both took. But for some time now, your liabilities have far exceeded your assets. Your loan payments are consistently late and interest is ballooning." Justine paused for Elena's response, excuse, remorse, anything. Defiant silence behind stony eyes was the obstinate reply.

"I read today's newspaper article on your land development problems," Justine continued. "It will be years before you see any return on that investment."

Elena loudly exhaled and flicked her wrist, as if backhanding an irritating fly. "The architect found a new builder," she said with a tone of weariness. "And if you've looked at the restaurant chain, the profits are picking up, even though we had to close a couple of locations. Don't worry," she added with sarcastic assurance, "things are going to turn around."

Justine tapped her ring finger on the desk. This was not going well. "Elena, this must come to an end. I can't authorize money for new investments when you haven't paid past loans." She rifled through a stack on her desk and withdrew a single sheet of paper. "The total loan package of your real estate, restaurants, dotcom investments, and international hotel chain is staggering. With interest, your current debt is six billion."

Elena stared. *Yeah, so? What's your point?* Then the force of the figure hit her. *Six billion. I didn't realize it was that much.* She did some fast calculating in her head. *Let's see, the restaurant launch was three million. My partners and I each put in a million for the plane and flight crew. The film production company was thirty million, but we acquired it more for prestige than profit. I can't even estimate how much we put in the dotcom craze. Okay, the hotel chain was pricey, but it has a guaranteed large return.* She mentally scanned her list of joint ventures and capital investments. *Yeah, it all starts to add up, but how does she get six billion?*

Justine watched as bewilderment contorted Elena's strong features. Perhaps if Elena saw it in print, she would understand the magnitude of the debt. "Would you like to see the numbers?" Justine extended the paper across the desk.

Elena lifted her hand, not to take the paper but to dab beads of sweat from her upper lip. *Think, think!,* she demanded of herself. *I can't let Justine back me into a corner. What did that* How to Win *book say? "Be bold." Okay, here goes.*

"Come on, Justine," she said. "This is the world of finance. You, of all people, should know not to panic when the market dips. I've made a lot of money for the bank over the years. You've 'seen the numbers,'" she mocked, "so you know good and well I can't pay it right now. Give it a little more time and it'll be all right." Contempt belied the tight smile.

Justine's eyes narrowed. "Yes, Elena, I'm aware you can't pay out of your company accounts." She studied Elena's ingrained arrogance, her polished insincerity, then proceeded. "Well, since you don't have the cash, I have a plan to offset the debt. Let's add up some other figures." She picked up a Mont Blanc and slid a yellow pad in front of her. "Let's see, your plane is worth about 6 million; your house in Aspen is valued at 2.1 million; your condo in Florida about a million five. You bought a new Mercedes this year; used, you could probably resell it for $60,000."

Elena's neck froze. Justine couldn't demand the sale of her private possessions. That was illegal. She inhaled to object, but Justine kept talking. "The bank holds the notes on everything you own, personally and professionally, so we can liquidate all assets. We'll take whatever we can collect, then the bank will write off the rest. Let's continue, shall we? I see your art collection has increased in value. Your townhouse is paid off, so that's a clear profit. Your real estate agent will help you find a new house in a more moderate price range. I'll call your brokerage company to authorize sale of your stocks and bonds. Even in this market, we should be able to recoup a substantial amount of cash. Do you still board the Arabians in Texas? Is the yacht still docked in Florida?" Justine hesitated to read the next item, but Elena's hostile glare spurred her on. "Didn't you recently transfer ownership of your parents' home to your name?"

The women's eyes locked for a couple of seconds before Elena's face fell like the last few grains of sand in a timer. "Oh, Justine, no!" she cried out. "You can't!" The yellow suit seemed to slide out of the chair by itself, the body inside limp and boneless. The shellacked red bouffant disappeared from sight. Justine hurried to the other side of the desk, nearly stepping on Elena's outstretched hands. Elena grabbed Justine's ankles, nearly tipping over the banker. "I'll repay everything, I promise," Elena sobbed. "Just don't take my parents' house. Please, Justine, please. . ." Mascara streamed down her cheeks, black tears peppering the irradiated silk.

"Give me time," she begged. "I'll do whatever it takes to pay back every dollar. But please, *please*, don't sell my parents' house. I'll find the money somehow, just give me a little more time. Not my parents' house."

Justine turned away, embarrassed and irritated by Elena's groveling. She shifted her gaze to keep from looking at the yellow mound quivering at her feet. She scanned the bookshelf, the objets d'art, the expensive knickknacks. Her eyes stopped on a beloved old photo. The wedding portrait of her mom and dad. She breathed in the memory of her mother's starched apron, the curls of wood shavings in her father's beard. Justine's eyes and nose prickled with emotion. She remembered weeping as uncontrollably as Elena cried now when her own parents' home was sold. Signing the deed of sale was as wrenching as signing the order for their caskets. Her heart ached; she would give anything, *anything,* to sit with them once more, to linger over the dinner table, to see love in their eyes, adoration in their smiles.

A sudden thought interrupted Justine's sorrow. *Impossible,* she shook her head. *Ludicrous. I couldn't do that.* But after a few minutes of consideration, she changed her mind. *Sure, I can.* And she could. Her personal worth was a mile-long parade of numbers. Comparatively, six billion dollars was a mere drop in her ocean of wealth. The idea pleased her more. *Well, why not?* She looked at Elena. *Maybe this will set a good precedent,* she thought. *Might even set a trend.* She smiled at the possibilities.

"Elena," she said. "Elena, get up." She supported Elena's elbow and helped her back into the chair, then put a napkin in her hand. Justine noisily shuffled papers on her desk to give Elena privacy to blow her nose and wipe her streaked face. Justine waited for the sniffling to stop before she sat in the matching client chair. She took Elena's hands into her own. "Elena," she began softly, "I know how complex life can be. We get distracted by this business of money. It's easy to become obsessed by the accumulation of things. We get trapped into thinking our portfolio defines our worth. We negate what's valuable, what's important." She paused. "Elena, it is possible to buy attention and affection, but not love. Not family. So, I have another plan for you. Refocus your priorities. Enjoy your parents in the remaining years you have with them; love your family. Forget about the loans. I'll write them all off. I'm offering you a zero balance. As of this moment, you are debt-free."

Elena gasped, skeptical of the tenderness, the kindness in Justine's expression. She jerked her hands away. "Is this a joke," she choked out, "a cruel joke?" Again tears flooded her eyes.

"No," Justine assured her. "This is no joke, Elena. You owe nothing. Now, go pick up Robert and your children, then have dinner with your parents." She stood, simultaneously lifting Elena out of her chair. She put her arms around the trembling woman in the scorched yellow and hugged her as if she were a sister. "Go home," she whispered in her ear, "go to your mother and father's house with your husband and children. Forget about money, Elena. Spend time with what's truly valuable in your life."

Elena struggled to speak. Justine answered, "You're welcome." Elena stopped at the door, glancing back at the woman who never ceased to amaze her. *My life will never be the same,* she thought. *Never.*

The Second Meeting

*Compassion is not weakness,
and concern for the unfortunate is not socialism.*
—HUBERT HORATIO HUMPHREY, 1911–1978

*There can be no freedom or beauty
about a home life that depends on borrowing and debt.*
—HENRIK IBSEN, 1828–1906

Elena rushed past Gabrie's desk, stumbled into the bathroom, and collapsed against a white porcelain sink. She stared at her reflection in the mirror, critical of the redness of her eyes, the swelling of her nose. *Dang it,* she thought, *I always look beat up after I cry.* She bent to splash cold water on her flushed face, then dried with a paper towel. She emptied her cosmetic bag on the counter and began to repair her makeup. *What just happened?* she wondered as she dusted powder across her splotchy cheeks. *What did Justine mean,*

"*You are debt free?*" She reapplied mascara. *How am I going to explain this to Robert, to my board?* She outlined her lips. *If rumor of this gets out, I'm ruined. No one will ever do business with me again. What does it mean that Justine forgave my debt? What's the catch?* She stuffed pencils, brushes, and compacts back into the bag, then sprayed two long bursts of Diamond Roses around her neck. *I'll pay her back anyhow,* she vowed. *If I don't, I'll be in debt to her forever. She'll own me, for crying out loud. Every time we meet, we'll both know that the only reason I have anything is because of her manipulative, little ploy. We'll just see who wins this one!*

Elena shoved open the bathroom door so hard it slammed against the outside wall. She lifted her head to a haughty tilt and practically marched to Gabrie's desk. "Would you please inform the driver that I am ready to return to my office," she demanded. "I'll wait in the lobby," she snapped on her way toward the elevators.

Gabrie told Kevin, "Time to pick up the diva of dollars. Wow, that must have been some meeting. It looks like Elena has been crying."

Elena threw her briefcase into the limo, stepped in, and slid across the seat. Kevin braced himself for a verbal assault. But there was no chatter, no manic lecture. Only the suffocating stench of roses.

Kevin glanced in the rearview mirror and wondered what Justine had said. Elena was still wondering herself. *What kind of a banker writes off that much money? There's something behind this. She's deliberately trying to ruin my reputation. Who does she think she is, controlling my business? No matter how much time it takes, I'll pay her back. I will not be destroyed by that woman!* She looked out the window. "Stop!" she screamed at Kevin. "Stop this instant!"

Kevin pulled the car against the curb. *Aw, I hope she doesn't throw up in the car,* he grimaced. Elena opened the door and scrambled out. "Wait," he called, but she was already on the sidewalk. Kevin jumped out and raced after her. "Ms. Holt, wait!"

She couldn't hear him over the sound of her own frantic voice. "Karyn, Karyn!"

A middle-aged woman in khaki pants and denim shirt stopped and turned, puzzlement wrinkling her forehead. Dull, graying hair, hung shaggy and limp around her tired face. Karyn's features only slightly relaxed as she recognized Elena rushing toward her. "Elena, what are you doing here?" she asked.

"We have to talk," Elena snarled. Karyn tensed. "What's wrong, has something happened?"

"No, nothing has happened, and that's the problem. Come with me," Elena ordered.

"Why, what's the matter?" Karyn asked as Elena practically dragged her to the car.

"Get in, we're going to the bank."

"The bank?" Karyn cried out. "I don't understand."

Elena maneuvered Karyn into the back seat of the limo, climbed in and slammed the door. "Take us back," she ordered. "Hurry it up!"

Kevin made a U-turn, perplexed by Elena's bizarre behavior. It wasn't hard to eavesdrop on the manic voice; the redhead was in a full-fledged tirade. "How much longer do you expect me to wait?" Elena interrogated Karyn. "I've been more than lenient with you. It's not like I haven't given you sufficient time. What are you doing with your money instead of paying me back? Obviously, not buying new clothes." Elena's cruelty whirled in the car like a deranged hummingbird.

Karyn dropped her head into her hands. *This is a nightmare,* she thought. How she wanted to strangle her former sister-in-law. *I wouldn't owe you money,* she silently raged, *if your brother had paid even a penny of child support or alimony. I wouldn't have needed a loan had he sent the checks he promised.* How conveniently her bridesmaid had forgotten why Karyn borrowed $10,000. Maddie, quiet, studious Maddie, needed a computer for college, not to mention money for tuition and books. Katie had outgrown her ice skates and needed a new pair before the state competitions; little Katie, who dreamed of becoming the next Michelle Kwan. *I'll remind you why I had to borrow ten grand,* she wanted to scream, *because my children needed to go on with their lives after their father abandoned us. I asked you for money so I could put a lease deposit on a condo, so my girls had a home to live in.* Tears trickled down her arms and dripped onto her khakis.

Elena smirked when she saw the wet splotches. "Sheesh, Karyn, get a grip. Just pay off your loan." Elena wagged her head. "Ten thousand is nothing, a trifling. I spend that much a year on flowers."

Karyn swallowed, wiped her face with her hands, then stiffly turned toward Elena. "I will pay you, Elena, every cent of the $10,000," her words clipped and precise. "Just give me some time and I'll find the money somehow. I'll ask my boss if I can work overtime and weekends. I'll add another $100 a month to my payment plan."

Elena's lips thinned. "I don't think so. I want the balance now. I'll sign papers at the bank to garnish your wages. Or you can put a second on your house. Oh, I forgot. You lease. Well, sell something or hit up your parents for a loan. You can call them from the bank." She turned to look out the window and smiled. She hadn't lost her touch. *If only power were capital,* she thought smugly.

The rims of Kevin's ears burned with disbelief. Elena was more like her sleazy brother than anyone could ever have guessed. The scandalous habits of Karyn's former husband were no secret. The entire city knew about his scams, briberies, and infidelities. His prolonged trial for tax evasion kept the gossip mill running at full tilt. Everyone was outraged by the not-guilty verdict brought in on a technicality, then horrified when, a week or so later, he filed for divorce to marry his mistress. The indignity was one more straw on Karyn's stack of embarrassment and shame. And now Karyn had to endure evil Elena. Kevin shook his head. *Elena has no heart, no class,* he thought, *none at all.*

The disgusted driver slammed on his brakes in front of the bank. He held open the passenger door and held his tongue. It was not his place to comment. One word from him and Elena would have him fired. He felt helpless watching the two women enter the lobby. *This is so wrong,* he fretted. *Who can stop this nonsense?* He ran to the front doors, then sprinted to the stairwell. The tall, young man bounded up the steps two at a time all the way to the third floor and nearly collapsed at Gabrie's desk.

"What is wrong with you," she asked. "Why are you running like a madman?"

"You have to stop Elena," he gasped. "She's in the lobby."

Gabrie frowned at him. "In the lobby? I thought you already picked her up?"

"I did," he shouted. "But she made me stop for her sister-in-law, well, her former sister-in-law, and bring them back!"

"Who? What *are* you talking about?"

"Listen to me," Kevin snapped. "Elena's making her brother's ex-wife pay back a $10,000 loan right now. She's forcing Karyn to sign papers and…"

Gabrie jumped up. "Did Elena tell you what Justine did in the meeting?" she fired at Kevin. "Do you know?"

Kevin lifted his shoulders. "How would I know?"

"Justine forgave Elena's entire debt. She wrote off *six billion dollars.*" Gabrie waited for the meaning to sink in.

Kevin stared at her, his chest heaving from his run up the stairs, his mind spinning with incomprehension.

"Follow me," Gabrie commanded.

Justine was startled when two bodies burst into her office. "What is it?" she demanded.

Gabrie began, but Kevin interrupted. Between the two, the story became clear.

Justine rose. "Kevin, are you sure you heard correctly?"

"Yes, ma'am, positive," he nodded. "Ms. Holt said she was going to garnish that woman's wages or make her call her parents for a loan."

Justine pushed a button on her phone and quietly spoke. "Delay Elena Holt until I get downstairs," she said. "Do not let her leave under any circumstances. And push the silent alarm. Understood?"

Kevin bolted toward the stairwell while Justine and Gabrie ran for the elevator.

Reaching the lobby first, Kevin positioned himself by the main entrance. When the elevator doors opened, Gabrie stayed behind and pushed the "hold" button. Justine rushed toward Elena and a visibly shaking Karyn. "Elena!" Justine called.

Elena's head popped up like a balloon surfacing from beneath a pool of water.

Justine stepped between the two women and held her hand out to Karyn. "Excuse me," she said. "My name is Justine Brooke, and I'm the president and owner of this bank. I'm sorry we meet under these unpleasant circumstances. Would you please wait for me in my office? Gabriella will take you upstairs while I speak to Ms. Holt."

Dazed, Karyn offered her hand to Justine, then walked in slow motion toward Gabrie. When she was within arm's reach, Gabrie pulled her into the elevator and repeatedly jabbed the "close door" button. *Drat,* Gabrie thought. *I'm going to miss the second power meeting of the day.*

The Third Meeting

As long as there is one upright man,
as long as there is one compassionate woman,
the contagion may spread and the scene is not desolate.
Hope is the thing that is left us in a bad time.
—ELWYN BROOKS WHITE, 1899–1985

Then there's amortization,
the deadliest of all,
Amortization of the heart and soul.
—VLADIMIR MAYAKOVSKI, 1893–1930

Justine was quoted all over the city. Tellers called their friends and family, bank clients reported to the media what they heard. People on the street, in offices, in bars, in backyards and living rooms applauded Justine's eloquence. "Finally," they cheered, "someone got what they deserved!"

Gabrie insisted that Kevin tell her everything. "Start at the beginning," she said, "and don't leave out a single detail!"

Kevin told her that about the time the elevator doors closed Justine turned to Elena. Her face remained calm, her voice stayed low, but her words were as sharp as rosebush thorns.

"You heinous woman. What a sorry excuse for a human being."

Gabrie shrieked. "Did Justine really say that?"

"Oh, there's more," Kevin nodded. "She was just warming up."

He told how Justine slowly shook her head as if to say, "Shame, shame!" Instead she said, "Do you think I wrote off your debt because it was good business? No, you ungrateful wretch. I was lenient because you begged for leniency, because you cried what I now think were fake tears. You've pulled one too many scams, you corrupt phony."

Kevin leaned in. "You should have seen Elena's face. It was as red as her hair," he chortled.

"Go on, go *on,*" Gabrie urged, punching him on the shoulder.

"Well, the berating continued," Kevin said, "and Elena shook like Jell-O."

He closed his eyes to recapture the image of Justine slamming her fist on the counter and shouting, "Why in God's name didn't you treat Karyn the way I treated you? You always try to act like everyone else, buy what they buy, go where they go. Why didn't you try to act like me? I forgave *six billion dollars* and let you keep millions of dollars worth of property. But you turned right around and tried to squeeze $10,000 from a woman who owns nothing, *nothing!*"

"And after that statement," Kevin concluded, "Justine turned to a teller and said, 'Call my lawyer and inform him what's happened here. Instruct him that I wish to file a suit against Ms. Holt on the grounds of falsified financial statements, willful perpetration of fraud, and misappropriation of funds. On Karyn's behalf, add kidnapping and extortion.'"

The pulse of police sirens signaled the end. A local news truck slid to a stop outside the front doors. Justine turned back to Elena. "I expect that you will now have plenty of time to ask yourself how you're going to repay six billion dollars, or why you were so cruel to Karyn." Elena didn't reply. She was too busy brushing wrinkles from her suit, preparing for the press. Even now she was lost in her own world of self-concern. Justine watched Elena's preening before handing down her own final verdict. "Don't worry, Elena…you'll look good in prison blue."

CHAPTER 4

The Parable of the Unforgiving Servant

❧

At First Glance

Matthew 18:21-35

Then Peter came and said to him, "Lord, if another member of the church sins against me, how often should I forgive? As many as seven times?" Jesus said to him, "Not seven times, but, I tell you, seventy times seven.

"For this reason the kingdom of heaven may be compared to a king who wished to settle accounts with his slaves. When he began the reckoning, one who owed him ten thousand talents was brought to him; and, as he could not pay, his lord ordered him to be sold, together with his wife and children and all his possessions, and payment to be made. So the slave fell on his knees before him, saying, 'Have patience with me, and I will pay you everything.' And out of pity for him, the lord of that slave released him and forgave him the debt.

"But that same slave, as he went out, came upon one of his fellow slaves who owed him a hundred denarii; and seizing him by the throat, he said, 'Pay what you owe.' Then his fellow slave fell down and pleaded with him, 'Have patience with me, and I will pay you.' But he refused; then he went and threw him into prison until he would pay the debt.

"When his fellow slaves saw what had happened, they were greatly distressed, and they went and reported to their lord all that had taken place.

"Then his lord summoned him and said to him, 'You wicked slave! I forgave you all that debt because you pleaded with me. Should you not have had mercy on your fellow slave, as I had mercy on you?' And in anger his lord handed him over to be tortured until he would pay his entire debt.

"So my heavenly Father will also do to every one of you, if you do not forgive your brother or sister from your heart."

A Closer Look

During a sightseeing trip in Israel, my husband and I purchased a three-foot long, twisted shofar to add to our musical instrument collection. The tip of the yellowy streaked ram's horn was cut off to make a small half-inch trumpet mouthpiece. The seller raised the shofar to his lips and blew out a long, loud note. Good to get someone's attention; wouldn't want to use it in an orchestra or band.

For thousands of years, Israel used the shofar to sound alarm, assemble an army, proclaim accession of a king. In ancient Jericho, God used blasts of the shofar and shouts of the people to bring down the city walls. This parable of the selfish servant reads like a shofar sounds. It's a narrative blast that crumbles the past and heralds a new way of living.

Why was such a dramatic note necessary? Jesus wanted the attention of his disciples. It is very likely that this parable of the Unmerciful Servant was told in preparation for the Day of Atonement. "The ten-day period between the Jewish New Year and the Day of Atonement was designated for seeking forgiveness between individuals. A person was not prepared to seek divine mercy during the great fast if he or she had not first sought reconciliation with his or her neighbor."[1] Individual forgiveness was a prerequisite for acquiring divine mercy. While the Gospel of Matthew does not mention the month in which Jesus taught this parable, Peter's question addressed an issue central to the time between Rosh Hashanah and Yom Kippur—the Ten Days of Awe (Teshuvah).

Peter knew that rabbis considered three times sufficient for the forgiveness of a repeated sin, and Jesus seemingly reiterates that number in the verses preceding the parable.[2] As the usual spokesman for the other eleven disciples, Peter asked Jesus how many times they *really* were required to forgive. Before he could answer, Peter offered a suggestion. "Seven times, right?"

Seven. Such mystery in a single numeric digit. Unlike ancient times when numbers rang with theological symbolism,[3] little significance is given to numbers these days. In the Old Testament, seven symbolized perfection, the creation, and the holy day of Sabbath. Every seven years, Jubilee was observed. Debts were to be forgiven in accordance with the Law. Every fiftieth year, after seven cycles of seven years, the blast of the shofar on the Day of Atonement launched the Year of Jubilee.[4] The year-long celebration of liberty and justice was designed to ensure that ancestral lands were restored to original owners, leases were expired, debts were canceled, and slaves were set free. Peter probably considered seven a generous number, ringing with jubilant tones of holiness. I can almost envision Jesus shaking his head at Peter's incomprehension. "No," Jesus said, "not seven times. Try seventy *times* seven."[5]

Peter's eyes widened as he did the math. *Forgive 490 times? Is that even possible?* No, it isn't possible. Nor was a literal number Jesus' point. So he told an exaggerated, almost humorous parable, "A King Wished to Settle Accounts,"[6] in order to emphasize that it's not how many times we forgive, but rather, *how* we forgive. What matters is the manner in which we receive, and then grant or withhold forgiveness.

Jesus began, "The kingdom of heaven has become like a king who wished to settle accounts with his slaves." The great Storyteller used the realm of finance as his setting. Many of his parables dealt with talents, denarii, wages, debt forgiveness.[7]

"Money," Jesus warned, "is like a master. And no one can serve two masters. You must pledge your loyalty to one or the other, but you cannot pledge to both. You cannot serve God and wealth."[8] Jesus knew that financial disputes can estrange families, friends, and business associates. To teach Peter and the disciples the value of forgiveness, he used the analogy of money.

Money was a weighty matter in the first century. Literally. The value of precious metals used as currency was determined by weight. The hearers of this parable would understand the weight of the matter had little to do with accumulated wealth.

After Jesus established the story's setting, a summons was sent. Being called to "settle accounts" affected a Hebrew sharecropper or a borrower in the same way that an envelope with the IRS or a bank's return address can evoke dread in many of us. The parable opened with an element of legality. The king had every right to call in his debts. A contract had expired and final payment was due. "Might as well start with the man who owes ten thousand talents," the king decided. "Bring him in."

Thousands were the largest numerical units used in antiquity; no millions, billions, or trillions. A talent was the largest measure, a weight of 75 pounds, used to certify the value of gold and silver. So Jesus' choice of ten[9] thousand talents stretched imaginations to a breaking point. In the first century, one talent was equal to 6000 denarii. A common laborer earned one denarius a day, a silver coin worth about twenty cents. If he worked almost every day of the year, it would take fifteen to twenty years to earn one talent.[10] The first debtor in Jesus' parable owed *ten thousand* talents, about *375 tons* of wealth. By naming an unreasonable amount of debt, Jesus prepared his disciples for unfathomable mercy.[11]

The first debtor was brought in. He was not asked to stop by at his convenience, not issued an engraved invitation, not sent a certified letter. The king dispatched some staff members to escort the man back to the palace office. As the debtor made the journey across town, I wonder if he suspected why the king wanted to see him. His social standing was not disclosed, but he certainly wasn't an ordinary laborer, not with a debt of that magnitude. He was either a state official, provincial governor, or influential man of great wealth. Without a doubt, he was "cunning, shrewd, ruthless, merciless, calculating, and political."[12] His single-minded pursuit of power was partially aided by his use of extortion and threats of imprisonment. His fortune grew from the fortunes of others, conceivably an ancient version of a modern junk-bond trader. But, he forgot two very essential truths: he was a debtor, and there is always a settling of accounts.

Jesus eliminated any story-stretching chit-chat and jumped to the crisis: "He could not pay." Well, *of course* he could not pay. No one could pay that debt. With dry wit, Jesus stated the obvious. The king, in an effort to recoup at least a portion of the debt, ordered the sale of the debtor, along with his land and possessions, wife, and children. The value of a slave ranged between 500 and 2000 denarii, so if the wife was a stellar cook and the five sons were strong or smart and each sold for top denarii, their accumulated worth was only two talents—a far cry from paying off the balance.

Wait a minute. The man owed ten thousand talents and had *nothing* to sell or cash in to reimburse the king? What about his savings accounts in Jerusalem Trust? What about the ranch, the herds, the farm, the crops, the barns, the silo? Where were those 375 tons of talents stockpiled? Did he think he was fooling the king? The king's swift and harsh judgment indicated the measure of his wrath: debtor's prison for the financier and his family.

Peter probably choked on this point in the parable. The Torah allowed for a man to be sold as a slave only if he could not make restitution for theft. Old Testament passages permitted the sale of children only to pay the debt of a deceased father. There were no legal grounds in Jewish law for the sale of a Jewish man; that abhorrent practice belonged to the Romans and Greeks.

When the debtor realized the king's verdict was no idle threat, he fell to his knees and begged for mercy. "Have patience," he pleaded, knuckles clenched to a desperate shade of white. "I will pay you everything!" When reality set in, he restated his original plea. "Now that I think about it, I *can* pay you. Just give me a little more time." Now he'll pay *everything*? It's a brash, laughable response. The impulsive promise of repayment is as preposterous as the outrageous amount of debt.

How long did the king allow the man to grovel? Long enough to allow for a change of heart. In a voice reverberant with compassion, the king said, "Get up off the floor. Your debt is forgiven." What kind of a king was this? A king who gave beyond what was asked, who granted more than was requested. This was a king proclaiming a private Jubilee: land was returned, debt was forgiven, slaves were freed. There is no record or proof that Old Testament Jubilee actually ever was observed, but here, with one act of forgiveness, Jesus made it a unique New Testament reality.

Peter had to be gasping at this twist in the story. The cold-hearted, cruel, profits-above-people king was a kind-hearted old softy? The implied lesson sounded like a shofar's long blast. Jesus showed Peter an image of God, an image of himself: a listening, compassionate,[13] forgiving, second-chance-giving King.

The parable could have ended there, a perfect illustration of Matthew 7:7, "Ask, and it will be given you." But the Storyteller was not finished. Peter and the disciples would learn that the king was not a "softy" but a keeper of justice and mercy.

The man relieved of his debt flew down the steps, through the doors, and out into the street. He breathed in the salty sea air and thought to himself, "I'm a free man!" His gloating grew with every step, "Jubilee, I'm free, I'm free!"

But, he thought, *I've always been indebted to the king. I knew how to deal with him, how to get extensions by paying interest, how to finagle accounts. I don't understand what that "forgiveness" was all about. What am I supposed to do now? Maybe the king can afford to throw money away, but I can't. If word of this leaks out, I'll look weak. No one can know. I'm a businessman and must keep doing business the way I always have.*

And there was his problem. He couldn't imagine a new way of a living. He didn't know how to navigate the unfamiliar world of compassion and mercy. The place where he once felt secure no longer existed, and he felt caught on a rope suspension bridge, bouncing and swaying over a great unknown.

At that moment, he bumped into a business associate, a man who owed him 100 denarii. Old habits don't die easily. The newly forgiven man put his debtor in a wrestler's chokehold, a variation of the Roman and Greek practice of a plaintiff making his own arrest by grabbing the neck of the defendant's toga and dragging him to court.[14] "Pay your debt, now!" he hissed into the accosted man's ear, a self-righteous injunction that honest men pay their debts. That's irony at its best, the cauldron of greed calling the kettle corrupt. But it was not funny to the guy turning red and gasping for air.

This unexpected plot extension caused Peter to do some fast calculations. *How many denarii in a talent? Six thousand. Ten thousand talents equals 60,000,000 denarii. The poor guy owed 100 denarii. The first debt was 600,000 times greater than the second.* Did the forgiven man even consider the disproportional amount when he ran into his associate? Hardly.

"Please," the poor man begged, "have patience, and I will pay you everything." For the second time, Jesus has us hear a debtor's plea for mercy, identical to the first but for one small difference: probability. The colossal debt could never be repaid. The lesser debt, equal to four months of wages, was payable. Did the poor man's request induce the same effect, the same result? Not even close.

The Six Billion Dollar Man hauled the Ten Grand Man toward the town's courthouse.[15] He had no intention of creating a payment plan or of forgiving the debt. "The forgiveness and mercy he received simply happened to him; they did not change his way of viewing the world."[16] At this moment, he thought only of himself—what he was owed, what he had the right to collect, and how others perceived him. He probably saw himself as a business Olympian, dragging the small-time borrower down the street before a growing audience of bystanders. This rather stupid display of mercilessness showed he had no understanding of the forgiveness he had received.

The people watching were outraged by the gross injustice and humiliation one man inflicted upon another. A couple of the onlookers worked for the king. They yanked up their robes and ran back to the palace. "You won't believe what we just saw," they breathlessly told the monarch. When the eyewitnesses finished their report, the king ordered, "Get that man back in here, now!"

Peter had to be rubbing his throbbing temples. What was Jesus doing? First, he answered a question about forgiveness with an improbable story of exaggerated debt. Then, he painted a picture of pardon as thoroughly overstated. The forgiven man stepped away from mercy and implemented a miscarriage of justice. Where was Jesus going with this parable?

Back to the king, that's where. Again, the Storyteller jumped to the punch line. "You wicked slave!" the king shouted. I imagine that the twice-summoned man stood in front of the raging royal with his mouth open, as if he had expected to hear, "Well done, good and faithful servant; you have not lost your edge."[17] He must have wondered why he was condemned for doing what came naturally to him, for behavior that previously brought him power and wealth.

The king clarified the issue. "I forgave all your debt because you pleaded with me. Why didn't you show mercy to your business associate in the way I showed mercy to you?" In effect, he was saying, "Even given your predisposition to view the world through the eyes of strict justice, you should have seen that the mercy which was 'right' in your case was also owed to your fellow servant."[18]

"Because you failed to show mercy," the king said, "you will be tortured until the entire debt is paid." Again, Jesus chose exaggeration, this time more severe than the king's initial threat. Why such harsh punishment? To show how seriously God regards relationships between members of his community. The extreme penalty indicated that "the servant violated something sacred; he shamed the king, violated his honor in some fundamental way. The great act of debt forgiveness was meant to initiate further acts of forgiveness."[19] When this did not happen, the original forgiveness was revoked and punishment was added.

How do we respond to such an extreme parable? Most would conclude that the first debtor got what he deserved. But the parable's emphasis is not on the king's mercy but on the debtor's lack of mercy. The example left for us is negative: "Here's what *not* to do; don't do as he did."

How did Peter respond? He must have wondered whether the parable addressed his question. What did this story have to do with the repetition of forgiveness? The king forgave the wicked servant only *once*. Certainly not 490 times. Or seven. Or three. Just once. Why would Jesus seemingly contradict himself by practically incinerating the first slave after one failure? Because forgiveness is not a matter of numbers with God. It is a matter of attitude. God set the example and expects us to follow it. He expects us to love as he loves, to forgive as he forgives, to show mercy and compassion as fathomlessly as he shows mercy and compassion to us. Each member in the community of faith is obligated to forgive as a response to the experience of forgiveness.

This was not the first time Jesus spoke of the conditional terms of forgiveness. During his Sermon on the Mount, he said, "Blessed are the merciful, for they shall obtain mercy."[20] It was reiterated in the Lord's prayer: "forgive us our debts as we forgive our debtors."[21] And finances are very much at the heart of this issue. Forgiveness of sin is inextricably woven with the forgiveness of debt. Not only are we to forgive sins, slights, slanders, and moral or ethical wrongs, we are to absolve monetary debts, especially when repayment will bankrupt, enslave, or destruct a family.

In Matthew 5:23-24, Jesus requires reconciliation between Christian brothers and sisters prior to prayer and worship of God. The Confession of Sin in the Common Book of Prayer asks pardon for "what we have done and what we have left undone." It is a fearful thing to hear Jesus say, "So my heavenly Father will also do to every one of you if you do not forgive your brother or sister from your heart."

Today, this parable is often used to teach about sin generally rather than financial debt specifically. But it is not accidental that Jesus used money as the object of his lesson. In the ancient world, unpaid debt resulted in slavery while forgiveness of debt insured freedom. Jesus knew the importance of both financial and spiritual forgiveness for the sake of financial and spiritual freedom.

The parable opened with a king who wished to settle accounts with his servants. *All* of his servants. "Presumably, therefore, he continued to deal with his other servants as he had dealt with the first, proclaiming a gracious release and forgiveness beyond anyone's wildest expectations or hopes."[22] Now, more than 2000 years later, we who follow Christ are members of that group of "other servants." As recipients of God's generous forgiveness, we are required, as a recent movie urged, to "pay it forward," to be as generous to another person somewhere down the line.

I wonder if Peter was thinking of a specific person or situation when he asked Jesus the question about forgiveness.

Did he have an uncomfortable or volatile relationship with a relative, a friend, a fellow disciple? We don't know what answer Peter hoped to hear, but Jesus put the responsibility directly on Peter, not the offender. After hearing the parable, did Peter forgive the one who offended him, doing what the unforgiving servant could not?

If we gave forgiveness as generously as the King, the result would be so loud the world would have to press its hands over its ears from the deafening blast of Jubilee.

CHAPTER 5

Looking Beyond Power

Behind the Image

I believe every person is formed in God's image. Not necessarily in our physical features since God is Spirit, but resemblance is possible in our character, thoughts, and actions. Humility, love, and kindness reflect the image of our Maker; arrogance, hatred, and bitterness distort the likeness to our Creator. Author Kathleen Norris wrote, "If we have ever been on the receiving end of an act of mercy that made a difference in our lives, we have seen the face of God."[1]

Justine, Elena, Karyn, and Gabrie represent a fairly complete cross section of contemporary working women—single career executives, married mothers, divorced sole-supporters, financially independent to financially strapped. In their lives we see the consequences of selflessness and selfishness, superiority and sacrifice, compassion and cruelty. The reflection of God, the King, is evident in the mercy of Justine. Contempt and greed, envy and ambition distort not only Elena's facial features but any resemblance to God.

Justine's extraordinary act of forgiveness set off a chain reaction that affected every woman in the story. Could one simple act of forgiveness on your part set off a domino effect in your world?

Justine—The King

Justine was an exceptionally good business woman. She took seriously her responsibility to run the bank efficiently, to oversee accounts personally, and to grant loans wisely. She kept accurate statements and monitored daily transactions. Nothing escaped her watchful eye.

As bank president and owner, Justine had the right to collect Elena's debt and the right to receive any monies from the sale of Elena's possessions. What prompted a change of heart? First, her knowledge of true wealth. Rich beyond imagination, Justine knew that money could never fill the void of relationships, never replace the loving embrace of a mother, never substitute for the tender kiss of a father. She knew that life's greatest treasures are the love and laughter between parents and children, the passion and commitment between husbands and wives, the bond and faithfulness of friendships that endure illness, separation, and time.

Justine's decision was also prompted by Elena's earnest plea. The power of emotion and desperation was enough to reverse the banker's earlier intention. Justine had no cause to doubt Elena's sincerity, so she granted the request with a generosity far beyond expectation.

The bank's business practices and its employees reflected the owner: efficient, honest, fair, truthful. Gabrie and Kevin, in the blush of adulthood and in their first "real" jobs, were influenced by Justine's character, obviously learning from their boss's example. When confronted with injustice, these two young workers, like the biblical eyewitnesses, raced to the one authority who would restore justice. Justine did not fail them.

This parable is also categorized as a "last judgment" warning rather than a suggestion of "do unto others." Some consider the story a threat, "forgive or else you'll be in big trouble." I believe emphasis belongs on the generosity of Justine who reflects the image of God by forgiving the debt of one who asks. She forgives not because it is good business or because it will ultimately serve her own interests, but because her heart is filled with compassion and mercy.

Elena—The Unforgiving Servant

This red-headed tycoon resembled the elite Pharisees who loved money,[2] who flaunted their power and prominence like preening peacocks. They flocked together in privilege and exclusiveness. Their relationships were not unlike many of our own social clubs, special interest groups, communities, and churches. "You may join, but only if you're like us in every way."

Dwindling checking and savings accounts do not always cause us to alter our customary lifestyles. How did Elena ignore soaring interest, falling profits, mounting debt, or approaching payoff dates? In the same way we ignore the reality of our own dangerous situations. We do nothing as our relationships become bankrupt or our spiritual lives bottom out. We hope and pray for the best and then crouch behind inaction with phrases like "God will provide" or "God will make a way." Masking inertia and irresponsibility with spiritual platitudes is easier than initiating change.

Elena could no longer pass the buck when everything was at stake—her family, her house, her business, her possessions, her future. Even then, she relied on her own resources. "Give me more time," she pleaded, "and I'll pay back the debt." She was like an ostrich sticking her head in the sand to avoid reality. No amount of extra time or effort would have helped.

Elena may have been surprised by Justine's debt cancellation, but she voiced no thankfulness. This was just another business transaction. And in her business mind, she swiftly found a new avenue of power. Elena exercised the right to collect from Karyn.

Only people who enjoy freedom exercise "rights." Few people in the world are so fortunate. A very real danger accompanies this privilege: When a "right" is wrongly defined or wrongly motivated, it can quickly become reckless, or at its worst, evil. Elena might argue that she did what Justine did. But she did not, because her motivation was selfish and cruel. Her legal right to ask for repayment became morally wrong.

Why didn't Elena forgive as she had been forgiven; why didn't she follow Justine's example? After her debt was canceled, she still had piles of money, prestige, and property, yet it wasn't enough. For some, the inability to forgive or show mercy is wrongly called good business practice. The will to own or exert control over others is lauded as "looking out for number one." For some, every decision, action, and motive is driven by an insatiable desire for more, like an addict's craving for a hit.

Obviously, Elena was not familiar with Jesus' words, "from everyone to whom much has been given, much will be required."[3] She was given great wealth, which she spent mostly on herself; she was given great forgiveness, which she did not replicate. "To receive forgiveness both enables and obligates one to offer forgiveness, not as an occasional exception to the rule but as a habit of life."[4] Elena's failure to forgive—something we think she should have done—had severe consequences. "Woe to you if you try to stand on your rights," wrote theologian Eta Linnemann. "God will then stand on his and see that his sentence is executed rigorously."[5]

Karyn—The Unforgiven Servant

Karyn couldn't seem to get a break. Her adult life was a string of disappointments, struggles, emotional upheavals. She was betrayed, abandoned, humiliated by those she once called family. Despite her former husband and sister-in-law's disdain Karyn refused the role of victim. Immense inner strength got her up in the morning and kept her working toward a good life for herself and her daughters.

Women like Karyn may buckle under those last straws of injustice but only briefly. They summon inner strength by the awareness of their responsibilities to others. They may have little, materially speaking, but have great wealth in relationships. Grasping this truth, we begin to understand what seemed a paradox when Jesus called the poor and persecuted "blessed."

Under immense stress, Karyn was consistent: a woman of her word, a woman who met responsibilities. She did not allow the opinion and criticism of another to alter her sense of self-worth. In the presence of wrong, she did what was right. Can the same be said of us? Karyn, the worn-out, sole-supporter of her family, was physically and emotionally tired of singularly paying bills, transporting children, cooking, cleaning, cheering, and parenting. Where do women like Karyn find encouragement, a supportive arm, a sympathetic ear? Who takes their side? Who intervenes on their behalf?

Elena and Karyn's perspectives couldn't have been less similar. Elena saw what Karyn didn't have—money. Karyn saw what Elena didn't have—empathy. Elena exercised her power, Karyn exercised her self-control. Elena gloated in her superiority, Karyn sacrificed for her daughters. Elena ultimately got what she deserved. Did Karyn?

We do not know what transpired between Justine and Karyn when finally they met. But we trust that Justine was as generous with Karyn as she had been with Elena. That is the hope of those who struggle through hardship, exhaustion, and unfairness. Indeed, it is the hope of all Christians that one day, when accounts are settled, immeasurable justice, mercy, and compassion will cancel all debts.

Seeing Ourselves

On May 13, 1981, Pope John Paul II was shot by a Turkish terrorist on St. Peter's Square. Almost immediately following his hospital discharge, the Pope visited the gunman in his cell and offered forgiveness. To the watching world, it was an incredible portrayal of Christ. In opposition to the international response of papal admiration, one person wrote in an editorial letter, "It's his job to forgive." Yes, it is his job. As it is ours. Forgiveness is in the job description for all who call themselves Christians.

When Peter and the disciples heard this parable, how long did it take them to realize that this was not a doctrinal lesson but an exposure of attitude? It is unlikely that they immediately identified with either of the servants. And only God himself could fill the role of the king. So where did that leave them? Where does it leave us? Which character most closely reflects our thoughts and behaviors?

Author Robert Farrar Capon suggests that there is only one unforgivable debt: "to withhold pardon from others."[6] The choice to forgive is ours alone. No one can forgive for us or on our behalf. We alone can offer forgiveness to those who have wronged us, or to ask for it from those we have wronged.

We who are "queens" of our personal domains may rule with nearly unlimited authority. We can impose inflexible standards on others, and the failure to meet them justifies punishment. How often do mothers exert the right to punish children by withholding allowances or sentencing combative teenagers to exile in their rooms? Is it easier to remain rigid even when a situation can benefit from mercy? What does a child, spouse, friend, stranger have to do or say to melt your heart, to receive compassion?

I know too many people who clench their teeth and mutter, "I will *never* forgive him/her for that." Some women go to bed at night, sleepless with hatred, anger, and resentment toward a former husband. The current social voice is weak in forgiveness but packed with vengeance. A character in a hit movie advised other divorced wives, "Don't get even, get everything." Jesus advised us to forgive everything; a suggestion easily understood but difficult to enact.

How much of our time is spent in the effort of acquisition? When is enough "enough"? Why do we think more and newer are better? Elena failed to value the non-monetary treasures of her life. What are our treasures, what do we value?

"We live in a culture where the ethos of forgiveness is not generally accepted or welcomed. Such an unforgiving culture is often reflected in our churches, where schism is more prevalent than unity."[7] Is this true in your church?

Gabrie had the courage to tell Justine about Elena's treatment of Karyn. Where is the fine line between meddling and intervention? What level of injustice spurs our involvement in issues that might be considered none of our business?

How can we exemplify this parable in our daily life, especially since few of us are rich like Justine? It's a wonderful gesture to secretly slip a $20 bill in a purse or send an anonymous gift certificate from a nice restaurant. And generosity is not limited to money. We can more easily give time and attention: we can baby-sit, mow a lawn, wash windows; loan books, dishes, clothes, a car; deliver dinner, take Christmas presents to the post office. All of these gifts give freedom, especially to a friend. But how much more difficult is it to give the gift of forgiveness to enemies, to those who have greatly wronged us? The king's generosity canceled a legitimate obligation; he forgave what seemed unforgivable.

In this story, it was hoped that Elena would renounce her former way of living. But it is not easy to change entrenched habits, traditions, or policies, even opinions, thoughts, and prejudices. Not in families, corporations, or nations. But one person can break the chain and begin a new pattern.

We who call ourselves Christian are to forgive as Christ forgives. The exaggeration Jesus chose as his point about forgiveness is as radical an idea for the New Testament as the year of Jubilee was for the Old. Both seem impossible. We don't know when, if ever, the year of forgiveness was actually celebrated in ancient Israel. Not many know that the year 2000 ushered in the third millennium and also the Year of Jubilee. Pope John Paul II, along with celebrities like Bono, lead singer for the Irish band U2, and some prominent world leaders, urged the United Nations, the United States Congress, the G7, and the International Monetary Fund to proclaim the Year 2000 a genuine year of Jubilee by forgiving Third World debt, an accumulation into the trillions.[8] Some mocked such an illogical proposal, others praised the concept but failed to put it into practice. Had they had the courage to proclaim Jubilee, what would have been gained? Would the benefit have trickled down to the poor, to small local communities? How loud, and how long, would the shouts of support reverberated around the world?

As disconcerting as it may be, a parable requires that we identify with a character in the story, that we examine our behavior, our attitudes, and motives. If you have abundant wealth and social status like Elena, how can your affluence, your prominence, positively or negatively affect others? Are your business practices the same for the rich as for the poor? If you once treated someone unjustly, can you rectify the situation?

Do you see your reflection in Karyn, struggling to hold your head up, guarding your self-esteem, your self-worth? Does it seem that the Elenas of the world are rewarded for questionable practices while you are penalized for doing what's right? How do you keep from becoming resentful, or becoming like them?

Justine, a parabolic Christ, was powerful, but not immovable. She overruled "business as usual" with unusual mercy. She intervened with justice when ingratitude and inequity played out in her domain. If you choose to identify with her, who is the first person on your list to forgive? A cheating spouse, violent parent, unruly child, dishonest employer, lying friend? Who are the on-lookers of your actions and how will your forgiveness influence them? To be like Justine is to be like God. Perhaps this is the day to begin to settle accounts, the day to blow the shofar of Jubilee.

CHAPTER 6

Reflections of Justice

❧

When Jim and I were newlyweds, which for us translates "poor," our decorating style could have been described as stark or minimalist. We were grateful for a new, extra-firm, California-king-size mattress and springs that Jim's parents gave us as a wedding gift. The bed, resting on a metal frame, and an old, hand-me-down dresser completed our bedroom furnishings.

A few months after our wedding, I saw a pewter and brass headboard for sale in the newspaper. I showed the picture to a friend at work, who agreed that it was beautiful. "Are you going to buy it?" she asked. "No," I sighed. "We can't afford it." She nodded with understanding. A few days later, she came to my office. "Here," she said, holding out a small envelope. "This is a loan for your headboard. Pay it back when you can." With a hug and a smile, she gave me a check for the exact amount. Jim and I happily bought our first piece of furniture and then stressed over paying back the loan.

I offered to make weekly or monthly payments, but my friend said time wasn't an issue. Not a single day passed without an awareness of debt. When I finally wrote the check to repay the loan in full, I breathed a sigh of relief.

Borrowing money, or clothes, or cars, or just about anything brings the possibility of a disastrous ending. Jesus' story of one friend owing another friend money didn't have a happy ending. Neither did the story Liz told me. Her mother,

Florence, was a woman willing to do anything for anyone, a woman who would give anything she owned to someone who might need it. Cautiously driving through drifting snow one wintry night, Florence saw a woman stranded by the side of the road. She pulled over and offered a lift. The stranger got into the car, shivering in her thin, frayed coat. Florence turned the heater up to high and over the noise of the fan chatted with her passenger.

When they arrived at a gas station, the passenger turned to express her thanks for the ride. Florence unbuttoned her jacket, took it off, and handed it to the woman. "Here," she said, "this will keep you a little warmer." The woman protested such generosity, but eventually accepted, gratitude obvious in her tears.

Florence hadn't given the stranger a worn-out jacket she kept in the trunk, intending to give to charity someday. She gave her own jacket, the one she had been wearing, the one she especially liked. That's the kind of woman Liz's mother was. Unfortunately, that kind of generosity attracts takers as pollen does bees. Takers, like Florence's cousin, Marilyn.

Liz was a teenager when her parents invested in a second home. When news of the purchase made the family rounds, Marilyn popped up like a jack-in-the-box, needing a place to live, volunteering to rent the property. Kindness overruled Florence's reluctance; she just didn't have the heart to say no to her cousin. Against her better judgment and with palpable apprehension, Florence accepted the first month's rent check and handed the house keys to Marilyn. It was the last check she ever received. Every monthly promise of payment was retracted due to calamity or disaster or some excuse. Again, Florence's kindness wouldn't let her evict her own kin, so Marilyn lived in the house, rent free, not for one month, not for two months, but for seven years.

Liz's parents were not rich and their kindness cost them. Encumbered with two mortgage payments, they fell behind on other obligations—so far behind they eventually forfeited the second house back to the bank. Still, they didn't vocalize any bitterness toward Marilyn, a relative who needed their help. Lesson learned, they figured. Any thoughts of regret were eliminated by the sight of Marilyn's children happily playing in the backyard.

Years later, Liz got a job in a nearby city and began to search for a place to live. Apartment rates were sky-high and even an individual room to rent was more than Liz could initially afford. As a final option, she called her mom's cousin who now lived in the city. After hearing Liz's predicament, Marilyn graciously invited Liz to temporarily stay in her home. A very grateful Liz had a wonderful time there, lingering at the dinner table, enjoying her second cousin's company in the evenings, going to church on Sunday mornings.

If the story ended here, it would be a beautiful example of how a person who had received mercy generously gave mercy when opportunity allowed. But it doesn't end here. Liz had been a guest in Marilyn's home for two weeks when she was presented with a bill for "room rent." She stared at the paper in shock, not only because Marilyn seemed to have amnesia—conveniently forgetting her own seven-year stint as a squatter—but because she charged *twice* the local going rate for a room!

Liz politely paid the bill, gathered her things, said her farewells, and left. It hurt her to think that a woman who had been treated so kindly by her parents could be so heartless. Charging rent might have been justifiable, Liz thought, if she had been there for months, if that had been their agreement, but after two weeks as a guest? Marilyn's seven years of rent-free housing seemed completely forgotten. Mercy was stopped in its tracks by ingratitude.

Liz wondered if Marilyn would have treated her mother in the same way. Probably not. Hopefully, Marilyn would have offered her hospitality as repayment. But, the parable of the Unforgiving Servant would not have required Marilyn to repay Florence. Rather, the debt of gratitude is to be repaid by helping out yet another person in need. The king expected the forgiven servant to pass along forgiveness when the opportunity presented itself, an expectation both the servant and Marilyn failed.

Most of us can recall occasions when a debt of one sort or another was or was not forgiven, or instances when we exercised mercy or the "right" to collect debts. Do your stories end with punishment and judgment, or with compassion and jubilation?

The Image
of Humility

Charlotte: An Honorable Worker

❦

The Transfer

If a man aspires to the highest place,
it is no dishonor to him to halt at the second,
or even at the third.
—MARCUS TULLIUS CICERO, 106–43 B.C.

Amid the seeming confusion of our mysterious world,
individuals are so nicely adjusted to a system,
and systems to one another and to a whole,
that, by stepping aside for a moment,
a man exposes himself to a fearful risk of losing
his place forever.
—NATHANIEL HAWTHORNE, 1804–1864

Susan stood and tapped her spoon against the water glass. "Ladies," she called, "may I have your attention?" Conversation tapered off and all eyes focused on her. "Thank you for coming tonight," Susan said. "I appreciate your continued work in preparation for the first Braden County Women's Conference. It's very encouraging that more than twenty churches are represented." She looked at the women with gratitude. "I don't know about you," she smiled, "but I'll volunteer to do about anything in exchange for a meal I don't have to cook or clean up after!"

When the laughter died down, Susan thanked the host church. "River Creek Fellowship has generously allowed us use of their facility for tonight's dinner as well as for the conference, which, by the way, is now only six months away. I am pleased to announce that Lily Sheradon is confirmed as our keynote speaker." Delighted "oohs" and "ahhs" accompanied the spontaneous applause. Susan paused and tightened her grip on the podium. "On a personal note, I am sorry to announce that my husband's company is transferring him to Chicago, and we'll soon be moving." During the collective groan, Susan took a drink of water, more to suppress her emotions than quench her thirst. This was harder than she expected. "Regretfully, I must resign as the Conference Coordinator and ask for a replacement. Most of the work has been divided among the committees, but one or two are needed to oversee it all. Any recommendations or volunteers?"

Almost instantly, Darlene's hand shot up. Susan inwardly cringed. *Not Darlene,* she thought. *She's volunteering just to hang out with Lily.* Susan scouted for someone else, anyone, to show any interest. No one. She reluctantly acknowledged Darlene's insistent waving.

"I can take over as the Conference Coordinator," Darlene declared.

"Oh, Darlene, it's such a big job," Susan said with convincing assurance, like a parent reasoning with an obstinate child. "Would anyone be willing to serve as co-coordinator so all the work doesn't fall on Darlene's shoulders?" She turned from Darlene's gaping mouth to the opposite end of the room where several women were urging a dark-haired woman to volunteer. Finally the brunette agreed and raised her hand. Susan smiled and said, "Thanks for being persuaded! Would you please introduce yourself?"

"I am Charlotte Brock," she answered in a low, pleasant voice, "from the Community Church."

"Glad you volunteered," Susan replied. "Could you and Darlene meet with me for a few minutes following the meeting?" Both women nodded.

The meeting progressed with reports from each conference committee: advertising and ticket sales, door prizes, programs, special music, lunch preparation, the liaison between River Creek and the conference. Convivial laughter and good-natured banter sped up the agenda. "That's everything," Susan concluded. "Why don't we close with prayer?"

The women exchanged farewells and gathered their purses and wraps. Susan picked up two bulging file folders and waited for Darlene and Charlotte with a mixture of relief and remorse. She was anxious to relinquish the responsibility, but not the actual work. She loved it when all the pieces of a special event came together. *I'm really going to miss being a part of this,* she admitted to herself. *I hope all the months of planning and effort I've invested aren't undone by inefficiency or personality conflicts.*

Charlotte approached from the right and Darlene from the left. Susan felt torn by which to greet first. She knew Darlene, so she turned toward Charlotte. "Thank you so much for volunteering, Charlotte," Susan said. "This is Darlene." The two women shook hands and simultaneously said, "Nice to meet you."

Susan handed a duplicate file to each woman. "Why don't you look these over and call me if you have any questions. My phone number and e-mail address are printed on the inside of the folder." Charlotte quickly agreed and Darlene said, "I think I can handle it." Her sarcastic tone was not misinterpreted by the other two women.

"I'll be in town, packing up, for a few more weeks," Susan said. "I'll help in the transition in any way possible. While you're both here, why don't you exchange phone numbers and e-mail addresses?" Charlotte took out a pen, waited a moment, then slipped the file from Darlene's grasp. She jotted down her information and handed back the file. Ignoring Darlene's obvious reluctance to do the same, Charlotte opened her own folder and said, "Tell me your number and address, and I'll write it down."

Darlene spit out the information like a ticked-off auctioneer. "Thanks," Charlotte said brightly, capping her pen. Darlene glared back before saying, "I'll call you if I need you to do anything." Her curtness was intentional, and all three women knew it. *Oh, no,* Susan silently despaired. *I was afraid this would happen.* "Darlene," she said with concern, "no one means for you to handle this all by yourself. As co-coordinators, you and Charlotte…"

"It's no problem," Darlene interrupted. "I'm riding with someone else, so I've got to go now. Thanks for the file," she said as she walked away.

Susan's shoulders slumped. "Charlotte, I really apologize…"

"That's all right," Charlotte interjected. "No apology needed. Trust me," she patted Susan's hand, "Darlene and I will work it out. Don't worry about the conference. You have a move to think about. I'll pray for your family during this transition."

Susan felt assured that Charlotte's offer to pray was more than just a spiritual cliché.

The Divide

*Be not swept off your feet by the vividness of the impression,
but say, "Impression, wait for me a little. Let me see
what you are and what you represent. Let me try you."*
—EPICTETUS, c. 50–120

*Humility is the most difficult of all virtues to achieve;
nothing dies harder than the desire to
think well of oneself.*
—THOMAS STEARNS ELIOT, 1888–1965

"Hello. Charlotte speaking."

"Hi, Charlotte. This is Darlene. Sorry it's taken me so long to get back to you. The weeks and months just kind of fly by, don't they! Well, anyhow, I was just going through Susan's file. Wow," she chortled a contrived laugh, "I had no idea there was so much to do. And you know me, I always tend to bite off more than I can chew!"

No, I don't know you, Charlotte thought. *But I think I'm getting a pretty good idea.*

"So," Darlene plowed ahead, "I divided up the list between us. I've already booked Lily Sheradon's flights and hotel room and confirmed them with her office. I'll pick her up from the airport and drive her around that weekend. Since all that will probably take a lot of my time, I'm sure you can handle the rest."

Charlotte knew "the rest" was overseeing everything and everyone else. "That's fine," Charlotte answered. "In fact, when I didn't hear back from you, I made a couple of phone calls. Remember Janelle? She chairs the ticket committee. Well, she told me that the owner of The Ink Spot offered to print the tickets at no charge and the flyers and posters at cost. Becky has sponsors for fifteen door prizes and a couple more pending. The sound technician for River Creek bartered his services for ten free tickets, which he's giving to his mom so she can bring her neighbors. Yolanda is rehearsing a choir with singers from each church. They'll open and close the day with special music. Phyllis Mason from Streams of Life will lead the praise and worship singing in the morning and afternoon before Lily's sessions."

Darlene stammered, "I…well…uh, you already know all that?"

"Sure," Charlotte modestly replied. "I e-mailed this information to you last week. I figured you were busy, so I followed up, like Susan asked. Is there anything else you'd like me to do?" Charlotte heard Darlene's indignation inflate across the phone line.

"No," she snapped. "I've got it all under control." There was a lengthy pause. "Well, there is one thing," she said, softening her tone. "I've been wondering if we should have a banquet on Friday night. You know, to welcome Lily to Braden County. We could invite the head of each committee." Darlene paused. "What do you think?"

I think you mean for me *to organize a banquet,* Charlotte thought to herself. "Sure, that's a possibility," she answered. "Is there a limit to the number of women invited? Where do you want it held? Who's going to cater it? Can the expense be covered by the conference budget? Do you want a formal meal or an informal buffet? Child care? Will you plan a program or make any official presentation?"

"Wow, that's a lot to think about," Darlene faltered. "Why don't you just go ahead and decide those things. Let me know the place and I'll bring Lily. Her plane lands around 6:00, so make dinner for 7:00. Thanks so much, Charlotte. Gotta run."

Charlotte hung up the phone. *Everyone on a committee should be invited,* she thought. *Chairs* and *members have all volunteered their time and effort; so they all should get to personally meet Lily.* She quickly jotted down a list, picked up the receiver and started making calls.

The Rearrangement

The only wisdom we can hope to acquire
Is the wisdom of humility; humility is endless.
—THOMAS STEARNS ELIOT, 1888–1965

It had taken all day, but the banquet room was transformed. Charlotte had been working since early morning, consulting with the chef, assisting the florist and her staff, staying out of the way of the decorators. Now, ten hours later, she stood at the entrance to survey the results. It was definitely worth the effort. Bland, beige side walls were concealed by a copse of ficus trees, each sparkling with hundreds of tiny shimmering lights. The front wall was draped with white silky fabric cascading in soft folds, washed in pale blue and lavender lights. The effect was stunning.

In the center of the room, wide, long tables were arranged in a squared, upside-down "U," and richly decorated with sixty place settings: twelve on each side of the left row of tables, another twenty-four on the right, plus twelve across the back side of the head table. Ornate candelabra lifted flickering candles, golden flames refracting in the crystal goblets and polished silver. The sight was as dazzling as a designer's display in *Architectural Digest*.

The sweet scent of spring infused the air, rising from individual bouquets centered above each china dinner plate. Petals of deep pink and red-orange rosebuds closely tucked together with yellow tulips and stargazer lilies glowed like stained glass against the stark white table linens; thank-you gifts for the guests to take home. Charlotte's thoughts turned to the woman who made it all possible. *I wish Diane were in town to see this!*

Very early in the planning stages, Charlotte had called her friend for some advice. Diane Magnuson was an enormously successful interior designer. Charlotte invited her to the banquet and conference, then asked for some creative and inexpensive ideas to visually spruce up the event.

"Oh, phooey, I'm out of town that weekend," Diane said. "I'm so disappointed I can't meet Lily, but I can still help decorate! You know what we could do?" She excitedly began to describe the picture in her mind, an exquisite room with an equally extravagant menu.

Charlotte began to laugh. "Uh, Diane, our budget *might* cover the cost of the lights on the rented trees," she said.

"Oh, too bad," Diane said. "The conference is so valuable for our community. And I love the idea of thanking the volunteers with a banquet." After a few seconds of silence, Diane said, "Listen, since I can't attend, I'd like to show my support by underwriting the cost of the dinner."

Charlotte immediately protested.

"Please don't turn me down," Diane insisted. "It will be my contribution to a great event. You can thank me by getting an autographed copy of Lily's latest book. Think that's possible?"

Charlotte was speechless, which Diane interpreted as a yes. "After we hang up," Diane went on, "I'll call my favorite chef over at the Royal Plaza. We often work together, and I know he'll give me a good deal on the banquet room and dinner. What's the date again?" Charlotte choked out the date, day, and time.

"Charlotte?" Diane asked. "I'd like to do this anonymously, okay?" Both agreed to secrecy, and Charlotte hung up, marveling at the kindness of Diane, the goodness of one of God's people.

Now the moment had arrived. Charlotte dimmed the overhead chandelier and moved toward the entrance. As soon as she opened the doors, women rushed into the banquet room, each one surprised by what awaited them. They hesitated, astounded by the beauty. Had they not seen Charlotte, they would have thought they had crashed the wrong party. Chatter and laughter swelled as they found their assigned seats. Becky and Phyllis futilely looked for their names until Charlotte approached them and said, "You're seated at the head table."

"Really? We are?"

"Yes, all the chairwomen are seated there."

Charlotte escorted them to their seats and then returned to the main doors and glanced at her watch. Everything was right on schedule—everything but Darlene and the speaker. Where were they? She crossed the room, pushed through the kitchen double doors and instructed the servers to carry in the appetizer.

High-pitched squeals broke out among the women as servers entered, balancing trays of enormous prawns cascading over the edge of sauce-filled cocktail glasses. Charlotte smiled. This was only the first course.

Next came a delicate endive, Anjou pear, walnut, and goat-cheese salad, lightly drizzled with a sweet-hot raspberry vinaigrette. Baskets of steaming sourdough rolls were passed up and down the tables. Things were going perfectly except that Darlene and Lily's seats were still empty. Charlotte checked her cell phone. No messages. No missed calls. What happened? No one seemed to notice their absence, but Charlotte was getting worried. *Have they been in an accident? Did Darlene forget the location of the banquet?*

She ducked into the kitchen. The main course couldn't be delayed much longer or it would be ruined. Her uncertainty was interrupted by the rain-like pattering of applause. Peeking between the kitchen doors, she saw Lily standing just inside the entrance, graciously nodding in acknowledgment. Darlene stood next to her, waving like royalty, as if the ovation was expressly for her. When the applause died down, Charlotte eased back into the room and gently took Darlene's elbow. Pointing to the head table, she whispered, "Your seats are the two in the center."

Lily leaned around Darlene and said, "Hello, I'm Lily Sheradon."

"I'm Charlotte Brock. Nice to meet you. I hope you didn't have any trouble getting here."

Darlene's cheeks ignited like roadside flares, and she jerked away from Charlotte.

"Oh, no, just a little confusion leaving the airport," Lily replied. "We're obviously late. Hope we haven't caused a problem."

"Not at all," answered Charlotte.

"There's no problem," Darlene snipped. "Let's take our seats. They're up there."

Lily followed after Darlene as Charlotte returned to hold open the kitchen doors for a parade of servers.

The guests gasped at the presentation of the entree: a large lobster tail beside a sizzling filet mignon, grilled asparagus tips and lemon zest on a bed of wild-mushroom risotto, julienne carrots sprinkled with fresh herb sprigs. This was a meal worthy of a pictorial spread in *Gourmet* magazine.

Relieved that Lily and Darlene had safely arrived and the women were enjoying themselves, Charlotte leaned against the door frame. Only then did she realize her shoulders were tense and her stomach growling. She took her own seat, the last one on the end, closest to the kitchen. From there, she could keep an eye on things and easily consult with the staff. She wished Diane could be there to see how wonderfully the evening turned out. *I hope I can remember every detail and describe how spectacular the room looks and how delicious the food smells,* she thought.

When a plate was set before her, Charlotte didn't hesitate at what to taste first. Definitely the lobster, butter-drenched. It was more than scrumptious. A bite of risotto next. She glanced up at the head table and quickly lowered her fork. Darlene was shaking her head in a troublesome "no." Lily apparently asked another question, to which Darlene shrugged. Lily's lips moved again. Darlene threw down her napkin, jumped up, and briskly strode past the wall of trees. A few steps away from the kitchen doors, she ordered, "Get in here." Charlotte followed.

On the other side of the still-swinging doors, Darlene began to rant. "That woman is asking me a zillion questions," she yelled, arms flailing in the air. "How am I supposed to know how many women will attend tomorrow or their denominational affiliations? Who cares who's doing the music or what the exact order of the program is!"

"Well, obviously Lily cares," Charlotte said. "Do you want me to speak to her?"

Darlene stared at Charlotte. "No, I don't want *you* to speak to her. I want *you* to give me the answers."

"Do you have a copy of the program with you?"

"No, I don't."

"Shall I get one out of my car so you can go over it with Lily?"

"Yes, go get one. And don't be obvious when you give it to me." Darlene stormed out of the kitchen.

Charlotte went to her car and pulled three copies from her briefcase. The day's schedule was printed on sheer parchment and tied with a ribbon to a sheet of floral stock. As inconspicuously as possible, Charlotte slipped back into the room and approached the head table. When she was within arm's length of Darlene, Lily looked up. "Oh, Charlotte, good," she said with a smile. "I have a few questions for you."

Charlotte blanched. "As a matter of fact," Lily said, "Darlene, why don't you scooch over and make a space for Charlotte to sit next to me so we can go over tomorrow's details."

Darlene's eyes bulged with indignation. Charlotte looked at the floor. Darlene pushed her chair back and stood. With an exaggerated sweep of her arm, she motioned for Charlotte to take her seat. The room fell silent as women watched the exaggerated mime. Charlotte quickly sat down. Darlene looked up and down the head table for another place to sit. Every chair was filled. She bent over, grabbed her purse, and bolted toward the exit. Her dramatic escape evaded no one's attention. Only after she disappeared behind a door did the guests resume eating and talking.

"I'm so sorry," Charlotte whispered, stricken by the scene.

"Don't be," Lily said. She twisted at the waist to directly align her eyes with Charlotte's. "I know Darlene wanted nothing more from tonight than to be seen with me." Charlotte searched Lily's face for a trace of annoyance, but saw only truth. "During our conversation in the car, it became apparent that Darlene wasn't interested in Braden County's women or this conference. Her involvement was just a means of hobnobbing with a 'celebrity.'" Lily shuddered as she pronounced the word. "I certainly do not consider myself a celebrity, and I don't appreciate being labeled as one. And our grand entrance? Darlene deliberately stalled to make sure we were late. Well, everyone saw her enter, which was exactly what she wanted. And everyone saw her exit." Lily paused. "Trust me, it didn't take long to figure out who had done most of the work for this event." She turned and began to scan the room.

"Are you looking for someone?" Charlotte asked.

"Yes, a waiter."

"I can get what you need."

"Not for me, thank you. They need to bring you a plate."

"Oh, no, I have one already. I'll just go get it." But Lily had already caught a server's attention and asked for Charlotte's meal to be brought to her. The server responded, "I'll bring a fresh plate from the kitchen," and scurried away.

Satisfied that Charlotte was taken care of, Lily asked, "Do you have tomorrow's program?"

Charlotte handed her a copy, ran down the schedule, and proceeded to give all the information Lily had requested of Darlene.

"I'm impressed," Lily responded. "Your attention to detail will allow me to specifically tailor my sessions for the audience."

Charlotte let out a sigh of relief. *Tomorrow is going to be a great day,* she thought. *Thank you, Lord.* She looked out over the room, grateful the women were being filled with good conversation and a good meal. Tomorrow, she knew, they would be filled in a different way.

As another plate was set in front of Charlotte, she said, "This is so wonderful. Tonight, lobster. Tomorrow," she added with a twinkle in her eye, "sack lunches."

Lily laughed. "As long as there are chocolate chip cookies."

The roomful of women erupted into giggles and clapping when the dessert trolleys were rolled in. No diets tonight! They were caught in the agonizing choice between crème brûlée with a dollop of apricot purée, chocolate mousse with ginger cookies, or a small fresh fruit tart with hazelnut whipped cream.

Charlotte smiled. It was worth all the hours of planning for this moment of pleasure. As desserts were being served and coffee and tea poured, Charlotte pressed her sweaty palms against the tablecloth. Darlene was supposed to do the next part, but it seemed she had left for good. A few women had searched the hotel for her to no avail. So the introduction was left to Charlotte. She stood and called for attention. "Ladies, ladies," she said. "I hate to interrupt your conversation or your dessert. We're so honored to have such a respected speaker and best-selling author as our guest this weekend. It's my privilege to introduce Lily Sheradon."

Spirited applause crescendoed as Lily stood. "Thank you," she said, "for such a kind welcome. Let me start by apologizing for my late arrival. Believe me, I would have been early had I known such a delicious meal was being served!" Lily looked over at Charlotte. "I'm grateful to this woman who spared us from the usual chicken dinner." The women cheered. Charlotte blushed, embarrassed by the attention, and wished Diane was there to take the credit.

When the room quieted, Lilly continued. "I know that conferences like this are possible only by the efforts of many volunteers. Some of you have worked for almost a year so I could fly in, talk for a few minutes, then fly out. Just doesn't seem fair!" she playfully stated. "Let me assure you," her voice turning serious, "it's my privilege to be in the company of such dedicated women and to be a part of such an important event.

"I think acknowledgment should be given to the individual chairwomen for their service," Lily said. She turned to the far end of the head table. "Would you please stand, tell us your name, your area of responsibility, and then introduce your committee members?"

Everyone was surprised by Lily's request. Then Janelle stood and introduced herself as chair of the ticket committee. "I'm so grateful for Abby and Gwen's help," she said. "But I couldn't have done my job without Charlotte's encouragement."

"I'm Phyllis Mason and I put the conference choir together. I'd like to thank Keesha for accompanying us on the piano and Jaycee for serving as music librarian. And I'm especially thankful for Charlotte's weekly calls to check in and pray with me."

And so it went. Woman after woman thanked their committee members and then made special mention of Charlotte. Each time her name was spoken, Charlotte cringed. *This is so unnecessary,* she thought. *I was just doing my job.* After the last chairwoman spoke, Lily rose again.

"This has been an incredible evening," she said, "and tomorrow will be a full day. Many of the women who join us in the morning will arrive with exhausted souls. They will be tired from a long week of work and worry. Some of them will limp in with physical pain or fear. I'll do my best to refresh them, to encourage them, and to teach them. But we've already had our first lesson tonight. We've seen how one woman's attitude influenced each chairwoman, who in turn influenced her committee, whose work will directly affect the women who attend the conference. Sometimes it's assumed that a good response is the result of the speaker's ability or presentation or personality. Truthfully, a good response is the result of women like you, and women like Charlotte, who begin with a spirit of service.

"So, let me assure you," Lily said, "that the results are now in God's hand. But tonight, let's thank Charlotte for her hard work and her example."

One by one, the women stood to applaud a woman who had never been publicly applauded, who never wanted the applause. A woman whose humble service brought her honor.

CHAPTER 7

The Parable of the Wedding Banquet

❧

At First Glance

Luke 14:1-14

On one occasion when Jesus was going to the house of a leader of the Pharisees to eat a meal on the Sabbath, they were watching him closely.

Just then, in front of him, there was a man who had dropsy. And Jesus asked the lawyers and Pharisees, "Is it lawful to cure people on the Sabbath, or not?" But they were silent.

So Jesus took him and healed him, and sent him away.

Then he said to them, "If one of you has a child or an ox that has fallen into a well, will you not immediately pull it out on a Sabbath day?" And they could not reply to this.

When he noticed how the guests chose the places of honor, he told them a parable.

"When you are invited by someone to a wedding banquet, do not sit down at the place of honor, in case someone more distinguished than you has been invited by your host; and the host who invited both of you may come and say to you, 'Give this person your place,' and then in disgrace you would start to take the lowest place.

"But when you are invited, go and sit down at the lowest place, so that when your host comes, he may say to you,

'Friend, move up higher'; then you will be honored in the presence of all who sit at the table with you.

"For all who exalt themselves will be humbled, and those who humble themselves will be exalted."

He said also to the one who had invited him, "When you give a luncheon or a dinner, do not invite your friends or your brothers or your relatives or rich neighbors, in case they may invite you in return, and you would be repaid. But when you give a banquet, invite the poor, the crippled, the lame, and the blind. And you will be blessed, because they cannot repay you, for you will be repaid at the resurrection of the righteous."

A Closer Look

This parable reminds me of my sons when they were very young. Every time we drove some place, they fought for the passenger seat, shouting, "Shotgun! Dibs on the front!" Their bickering escalated for months before I came up with a solution. "You," I pointed to the elder, "get the front seat for the entire month." He grinned in victory. "And you," I pointed to the younger who sported a trembling chin, "get to sit next to me all next month." I looked back and forth between them. "Even months for you, odd months for you. And no exceptions!" From then on, if we drove half a mile or half a day, the "child of the month" felt privileged. The two boys quickly learned the difference between "even and odd" and paid close attention to the calendar! A simple solution ended the mad dashes to the car, the calling "dibs" an hour before departure, the shoving and elbowing for the coveted seat.

In this parable, adult men scrambled for the best seat next to the host, the softest cushion closest to the food. Jesus' solution to their competition was a retelling of Proverbs 25:6-7: "Do not put yourself forward in the king's presence or stand in the place of the great; for it is better to be told, 'Come up here,' than to be put lower in the presence of a noble." Jesus' etiquette lesson to the guests included an alternative. Instead, sit down at the lower end of the table, so when your host comes, he'll say to you, "Friend, move up higher." Then you will be honored in the presence of all the guests. The simple selection of a chair could determine the polarity of honor and shame.

Exalt yourself, Jesus paraphrased, and you'll be humbled. Humble yourself and you'll be exalted. The ancient proverb summarized the consequence of choice. Jesus concluded with prudent advice: If you want the other guests to notice you, take a lower seat and allow the host to move you forward. True humility never demeans and never assumes entitlement.

Jesus shifted his social scolding from the guests to the host: Don't invite your usual friends, relatives, or rich neighbors to an extravagant meal. They'll just invite you to their house in a cycle of repayment. Instead, invite the poor and the physically imperfect because they cannot offer a reciprocal invitation.

Shock captured the host's face. "Invite *WHOM?* To *my* house? You've got to be kidding!" Extending a party invitation to such flawed individuals was ridiculous. Such people were excluded from all significant community or religious leadership. First-century[1] Pharisees stressed holiness, especially when eating together. Gentiles, sinners, or other "unclean"[2] guests would threaten the purity the Pharisees were trying to maintain. Their presence would defile the whole meal and be considered as perverse as defilement of the sanctuary.

Jesus adamantly opposed the prevailing belief that only a chosen few would dine with the Messiah, that only the religious elite would sit around the table, laughing at the expelled Gentile kings, officials, and landlords. He was appalled that codes of nationalistic and religious purity controlled the guest list. Apparently, the host and the people of

Israel had forgotten, or purposely ignored, the prophet Isaiah's declaration, "On this mountain the Lord of hosts will make *for all peoples* a feast of...rich food filled with marrow, of well-aged wines strained clear."[3] So Jesus eliminated all exclusive restrictions by saying, "people will come from east and west, from north and south, and will eat in the kingdom of God."[4]

Banquets and meals were significant events in Jesus' life.[5] Where he ate, and with whom, garnered unprecedented attention. His eating habits[6] were so flagrant, it caused his detractors to complain, "This fellow welcomes sinners and eats with them."[7]

Then as now, feasts, dinners, and weddings were significant social occasions with carefully assigned seating. The best seats were reserved for the most important guests by distinction of age or social rank. Favored guests usually arrived late so their "grand entrance" ensured notice as they were escorted to their seats.

Ordinarily, three wide couches were placed at a table, one at each of three sides of a square; the fourth side was left open for the servants to present the food. Three guests reclined on each couch with their heads near the table and their feet stretched out toward the back. Their left elbows rested on a cushion to support the upper part of their body and their right arms remained free for eating. Since no serving utensils were used, the washing of hands was not only a required ritual but a matter of sanitation. Guests used their right hand to scoop food from dishes and to hold a piece of bread to soak up juices or pick up morsels of food. The three positions on each couch were termed highest, middle, and lowest, the best being the one with no one behind.

From earliest recorded history, eating and drinking provided the context for social ceremonies and meaningful conversation about politics, philosophy, theology, and most certainly gossip. A common setting "for philosophical discussions in Hellenistic literature was the banquet."[8] After a lavish meal, a lively symposium allowed Greek men to share drinks and intellectual discussion. So important was the combination of conversation and food that moralist Plutarch (c. 46-120) wrote six books titled *Table Talk*. Rivalry was so intense among the nobles that a Roman was not considered a luminary "if he did not at least once in his life pay for a public building or banquet."[9]

Before his death around the year 112 A.D., Latin author and orator Pliny the Younger criticized the discriminatory meal practices of one of his hosts.[10] Pliny and a few other distinguished guests were served very elegant dishes while the lesser guests were served cheap and paltry fare. Three flagons of wine were set on the table, the best poured only into Pliny and the host's glasses. Friendship was measured according to the degrees of quality.

In contrast, Jesus considered meals as occasions for inclusive celebration. He ate with all levels of society, disregarding customs and pretensions. The seating arrangements at this particular Sabbath meal provoked his scathing commentary. But the scrutiny began before he even arrived. Jesus and the other guests were walking to the host's home when they encountered a man with dropsy, a serious fluid-retention condition now called edema. He turned to his companions and asked, "Is it lawful to cure people on the Sabbath, or not?" They refused to get trapped by a trick question. Sabbath healing wasn't allowed unless a life was in danger. Dropsy, eventually life threatening, was not, in this case, imminently fatal. Jesus' question forced them to choose between adherence to traditional law or compassionate healing. They remained silent. Jesus reached out, touched the man, healed him, and sent him on his way.

Then Jesus posed a second question to his fellow guests: Wouldn't you immediately pull out your own child or your ox that had fallen into a well on the Sabbath? To modern sensibilities, the answer is "Yes, of course!" But it was not such an easy question for the Pharisees to answer. The written law of

Moses stipulated that an animal in distress could be helped, but it wasn't clear if this could be done on the Sabbath. The strict sect of Essenes left beasts in the pit. However, oral tradition allowed for emergency situations on the Sabbath. Jesus' healing defied tradition and authorized human precedence over Sabbath observance. We don't know if the man with dropsy was a stranger on the road or a member of the host's family. It certainly didn't matter to Jesus. He healed the man, changing his status from "unclean" to "clean," from unwelcome to welcome at an inclusive table.

I assume that the atmosphere was tense, or even antagonistic, when the guests claimed their seats in the host's home. It appears that they intentionally distanced themselves from Jesus and hurried to recline beside the knee-high table. The seating arrangement for this specific meal was not spelled out, but usually the host assigned the proper placement. If guests were left to seat themselves, as it appears in this story, their choices exposed their sense of self-importance.

Jesus stood back and humorously watched the men scramble for the best seats, most likely leaving a "lesser" seat for the radical Sabbath healer. I wonder if he waited until the first course was served before chastising the guests, waited until their mouths were full of couscous before criticizing their inhospitality. Jesus' advice to take a lower seat would have been considered absolutely crazy, a complete undermining of their position in the community.

Jesus didn't give much credence to one's position. He publicly scorned the scribes and Pharisees who loved "the place of honor at banquets and the best seats in the synagogues."[11] But then, bickering for a prominent seat was not confined to the religious elite or the wealthy. Even Jesus' disciples wanted better seats.

Brothers James and John privately asked Jesus, "When you're in your kingdom, please let one of us sit on your right and the other on your left."[12] I can only imagine the astonishment on Jesus' face upon hearing such an impertinent request. He looked into their pleading eyes and quietly said, "You have no idea what you are asking. Are you willing to suffer and die in the same manner that I am?" The brothers assured him of their loyalty. "Yes, we are! We are able to do whatever you do!"

I picture Jesus gravely shaking his head as he confirmed their future. "Yes, indeed, you will suffer and ultimately die for my sake. But the privilege to sit at my right or at my left is not mine to grant. That decision is left to God." Did the brothers walk away with their shoulders slumped in rejection? Did they understand the severity, or reality, of what Jesus just told them? Had they forgotten Jesus' caution that those who exalt themselves will be humbled?

Details of James and John's private conversation somehow leaked to the other disciples, who angrily reacted to the brothers' request. The confrontation must have escalated into a shouting match because Jesus summoned all twelve to address the issue. "You know that foreign rulers lord over their servants like tyrants," he said. "But don't you act that way. If you want to be great, you must be the servant of all others. If you want to be first, you must be a slave to everyone else. For I came not to be served but to serve, to give my life to rescue many people."

Leonardo daVinci's painting of the Last Supper is nothing less than a masterpiece by all accounts, but it's inaccurate in its lopsided seating arrangement. We know that John, "the one whom Jesus loved," reclined next to Jesus. Was his brother James nearby? Where were brothers Peter and Andrew? Judas must have been within arm's reach because Jesus was able to hand him a piece of bread.[13] Did John eagerly plop beside Jesus, or was he invited to take the seat by his Teacher? Since Judas was the treasurer, did he always sit higher than, say, Bartholomew or Philip? Even among the twelve, there seems a likely hierarchy. Regardless of where they belonged at the table, James and John wanted the two most important seats next to Jesus once his kingdom was established. If the twelve closest friends of Jesus fought for position, is it any wonder that the striving for place continues to be a common human characteristic?

As he often did, Jesus used an ordinary life situation to suggest extraordinary alternatives. First, he said, allow others to determine the public perception of your significance. Save yourself the embarrassment of humiliation by the demeanor of humility. Then, learn what it really means to be truly hospitable. The more the merrier at any feast that honors God.

Jesus, in the parable, asks us to make room for everyone at the table and allow God to determine who is placed in the seats of honor.

CHAPTER 8

Looking Beyond Esteem

Behind the Image

About once a month, my husband and I join four other couples in a food club for an international dinner. We choose recipes from a specific country or region, and then each couple brings one course of the menu. We've steamed, baked, boiled, and stir-fried dishes from Vietnam, Morocco, Mexico, Italy, France, and Eastern Europe. And, of course, we grilled beef, chilled watermelons and stuck sparklers in chocolate cake for the all-American barbecue on the Fourth of July. On the appointed night, we arrive at one of our kitchens with bulging grocery bags, utensils and serving dishes, pans wrapped in tea towels, and proceed to chop, mix, sauté, and sneak tastes of exotic food. Then we crowd around a table loaded with platters to finish stuffing ourselves.

It doesn't matter where we sit. At any place around our tables, the conversation is lively and loud. We toast promotions and job changes, emphatically voice opinions, applaud achievements and milestones. We laugh until our sides hurt and weep with unashamed emotion when sorrow spills out of us. Even though our friendships span eight to twenty-two years, the ten of us are closer since we started eating together on a regular basis. The table has become a place of honesty, celebration, comfort, and acceptance. It's a place where we know we belong.

I realize that not everyone experiences such camaraderie. Minor and major barriers can prevent such intimacy at a meal. Martin Luther King, Jr. dreamed that "the sons of former slaves and the sons of former slave owners will be able to sit down together at the table of brotherhood." That dream has only partially come true.

In this parable of the wedding banquet, two major observations are unavoidable. First, Jesus wanted the invitation list to go well beyond the people usually found in our company. It is almost as if he said, "I understand hospitality among peers. But, I am interested in your hospitality in the company of *my* friends: the poor, the crippled, the lame, and the blind."

The second observation is of place. The ten members of our food club have only one place: in each other's way. We are generally elbow-to-elbow in the kitchen, assembling ingredients, reaching for appetizers, pouring drinks. At the table we are equals—in appetite and relationship. Where we sit is not important. But, what if it were otherwise? What if, as Jesus noticed, one of us needed to feel superior, wanted the "head" seat, or insisted that our dish be especially praised before a serving spoon ruined the aesthetic presentation? Then, our unity would collapse, our inattention to status, shattered. Jesus was concerned about relationships when he observed the vying for position among guests at a dinner. From their conduct, he drew one of life's most demanding and most rewarding lessons: "All who exalt themselves will be humbled and those who humble themselves will be exalted."

Susan—The Visionary

Susan opened the story with a common conflict: a physical household move from security to the unknown. She loved being coordinator of the women's conference, but her husband's job transfer required her resignation. Her significance in the community was ending for a justifiable reason but that did not ease the sorrow of change.

Like many organized women, Susan feared that her months of planning and hard work might be undone or allowed to fall between the cracks by a coordinator less dedicated to detail. She reluctantly handed over files that contained not only her notes and lists but her dream. She wasn't resigning from a job but relinquishing a goal.

Susan knew that within a few months she would live in a new home in a new city, re-establishing order and beginning new friendships. But at that moment, she was concerned that an event deeply imprinted with her own intent would be passed to women who might or might not share her sense of vision. Initiators usually are creative and energetic but must often be willing to hand their dreams to others, to implementors. I cannot help but wonder if Jesus didn't feel some of this same concern, knowing how little time he had to initiate the work of faith, leaving his mission to a group of men who did not yet fully understand his intent.

Darlene—The Ambitious Host

I have seen several variations of the same cartoon. A slim, attractive woman looks in the mirror and says, "I have to go on a diet." An overweight, balding man looks in the mirror, flexes his flabby arms, sucks in his belly, and says, "What a hunk!" Darlene was an exception to the generality. She was quite self-impressed and more than confident of her importance, always quick to seize any occasion that could be manipulated for her benefit. Never mind that she may not have been qualified as a coordinator. She had one aim and one only—to be noticed. The opportunity to hobnob with a well-known author overwhelmed any sense of duty or reality. Volunteering was a means to an egotistical end, an impulsive response without regard to requirements or responsibility. Or is it possible that she was so insecure, she grasped for any and every occasion to bolster her self-esteem?

Darlene bristled at Susan's suggestion of a co-chair because obviously she didn't want to share the limelight. She enforced her superiority by intimidation, her intentional rudeness an unwitting validation of a principle written by Goethe over 200 years ago, "A man's manners are a mirror in which he shows his portrait."

Under an arrogant act of delegation, Darlene kept the important tasks and assigned the grunt work to others, a practice still evident among people in offices, schools, churches, and even families. However, with enough time, blustery women like Darlene usually are exposed through missed deadlines, inaccurate reports, unintentional self-exposure. In the evidentiary glare of incompetency, excuses are vocalized, blame shifted. In the style of many who are expected to be team workers, Darlene treated her co-coordinator as an assistant. Charlotte did all the work; Darlene planned to take all the credit. The banquet proposed as a "thank you" for the volunteers was merely a stage for her grand entrance with the guest of honor. She couldn't envision herself comparing printer's bids or soliciting door prizes, but arriving with Lily was vivid in her mind, down to the last detail.

What should have been her night of triumph became a night of humiliation. Darlene made her grand entrance, basked in the burst of applause, and claimed the seat she felt she rightly deserved. Her dream came true, until responsibility severed that brief moment of glory.

Once her self-serving purposes were clear to Lily, once the masquerade failed, honor vanished. The attention she so hungrily craved was now riveted on her lack of preparedness, her low regard for the event as a whole, and for the women who organized it. There was no one to blame for her lack of knowledge, no one to accuse of undermining her authority, no one to rescue her.

Darlene got what she wanted from Lily, but she had not expected Lily to want something of her. Clearly one thing and one thing only drove Darlene. She meant to be the center of attention, and she certainly had it in this moment of disgrace. Useless and without a concern beyond herself, she was politely asked to vacate her chair. Nothing was worse than the loss of power and place. Exposed and humiliated by Lily's request that she "move down," Darlene fled the room. Flight was preferred to the admission of failure.

Charlotte—The Gracious Host

Charlotte's friends knew she was an ideal candidate for conference coordinator and urged her to volunteer because her capabilities and talents were perfectly suited for the position.

In quiet confidence, Charlotte oversaw the weekend's every detail with careful concern. The women she worked with mattered more than the work they were doing. Her weekly phone calls were not like a supervisor's checkup, but the extension of genuine care and friendship.

In almost all industries, it seems that someone knows someone, and favors are done. Charlotte called Diane, a designer who took a nice idea and made it spectacular. Anonymity allowed Diane the freedom of fun and extravagance and eliminated any future requests for favors.

Charlotte expanded Darlene's original guest list of only the chairwoman of each committee and invited all the volunteers to the same banquet, serving the same menu on tables set with identical china, silver, and crystal. Other than the head table reserved for the chairwomen, everything else—from the exquisite settings to delicious food—was presented with equality.

Charlotte determined to anticipate and resolve problems before they occurred. Taking the last seat by the kitchen doors was not a self-deprecating assignment or a strategic maneuver for recognition, but an efficient, responsible choice. So when the compliments and adulation began,

Charlotte was embarrassed. She deserved, but did not expect, such an outpouring of admiration.

Lily—The Guest of Honor

Over the years of public life, Lily had made an uneasy truce with the fawning and flatteries of hosts attempting to make her feel welcome. She could not tolerate those who exaggerated their own status or importance by association with her. For Lily, meeting women in cities and towns across the country was a privilege, an opportunity to enjoy the company of new friends, if only for a day or two. Mostly, she considered herself a contributing member of a group committed to a common goal.

Lily's sense of contribution began the moment she was met at the airport. She felt it important to establish an immediate bond with the hosts and gave her undivided attention to their stories, laughed at their family anecdotes, and listened to the surgical procedures that always seemed to be told. On this day, however, barely had she buckled her seatbelt before she realized this was no ordinary host driving her to the hotel. When Darlene launched into an unending monologue about her own achievements and began to disparage her small county and its hardworking residents, Lily knew she was in the company of a self-serving woman. Whenever possible, she tried to redirect the topic, but Darlene, the talker and never the listener, missed every hint.

Lily preferred to arrive at a venue early and greet women as they arrived. She wanted to hear the voices of the women, to sense the personality of the group. Unless absolutely unavoidable, showing up late not only denied her that connection, but seemed to her arrogantly rude. When Darlene's deliberate dawdling ensured that they arrived at a banquet already in progress, Lily knew that, short of a firm confrontation, Darlene would continue to manipulate for her own sake. Once seated at the table, she made it clear to Darlene that she would not be late for Saturday's conference and then inquired about the next day's schedule.

As she always did in such circumstances, Lily asked for details about the time and length of the program. Darlene's ignorance and undisguised apathy was the final straw. Lily gently but politely asked her to move in order for Charlotte to be seated next to her at the table.

In Lily's final scene, we see a woman who took charge of a situation spiraling out of control. She took the reins and redirected the attention back to the volunteers, back to the purpose of the conference. Lily was a guest of honor who diverted attention from Darlene to Charlotte and the women who so diligently worked on the weekend conference. Lily is the perfect example of an "exalted" guest who honored other guests as her equals.

Seeing Ourselves

In Mary's Magnificat, we again see a correlation between seats and food. We can only imagine the shock her words caused in the first-century where class, privilege, and social position were rigidly protected. In one powerful and quiet theological phrase, she completely reversed the usual order: "He has brought down the powerful from their thrones, and lifted up the lowly; he has filled the hungry with good things, and sent the rich away empty."[1]

Even when we don't give much thought to it, our position at a variety of tables indicates whether we are in a superior or inferior pose. Our sense of power and sometimes our security depends upon where we find ourselves seated. A doctor's examination table makes us subject to his authority. One seated at a school desk is "lower" than the instructor. Some families separate children from adults at holiday meals, where the head of the grown-up table is reserved for an elderly patriarch or matriarch.

Most of us can identify with the fictional characters in this banquet parable. A move or transfer, job loss or change, can drastically affect us. Like Susan, it can be difficult to "move on" when leaving a comfortable, secure position. Do we relinquish our work to those who follow after us with a blessing or an air of reluctance? Do we assume they'll never fill our shoes, or do we equip them for success? How do we react when "our" idea or dream improves in the hands of our replacement?

The Darlenes of the world rarely recognize themselves. They consider themselves the best at everything. And if they're not, but have any savvy at all, they hire someone to do the job without relinquishing the position of authority. Power-hungry or overly ambitious women are highly insulted when faced with the truth of their shortcomings. Why is it so difficult to admit our weaknesses? Do we run away when we're wrong, disappear when we fail or make mistakes?

In Charlotte, we see an example of "those who humble themselves will be exalted." Where do we see true humility in contemporary societies governed and distinguished by class or caste; where citizens are segregated in mansions or ghettos, condos or shanty towns; where language or accent divide as effectively as electronic gates and wire fences; where the physically beautiful are idolized in media and the physically impaired are pitied for their imperfections? Where, and when, do the exalted trade seats with the humbled? What circumstance brings equality to a world fraught with inequality?

Lily correctly redirected the conversation at the close of the banquet. No doubt, the room was buzzing with speculation on Darlene's dramatic exit. But Lily shifted their attention to the purpose of the conference: unity among women and maturity of faith. She knew there was a correlation between how we promote ourselves before others and how we promote ourselves before God. The advice that allows us to avoid humiliating shame in a social situation applies to entering into the presence of God. We enter with humility and wait for "God [to] lift up the head of the one who approaches with downcast eyes."[2]

Taking the "lowest place" means to appropriately recognize ourselves. It means being willing to see our failures and haughtiness, as well as our accomplishments and modesty. In the context of a spiritual banquet, we should be grateful that our names are on the guest list. The good news of the parable is that we are not invited on the basis of achievement or popularity, but to enjoy the company of the host and his other guests.

How should we incorporate the truth of this parable in our private and professional lives? What is the main topic around the dinner table, in the presence of our children? When we entertain, do we allow table conversation to slip into slanderous gossip? Do we mock those excluded from our company, people we would never invite into our homes for a snack, much less a feast?

On the afternoon of Jesus' resurrection, the first Easter day, two disciples were walking from Jerusalem to Emmaus, a nearby town. They placed one heavy foot in front of the other, shoulders slumped in despair. A stranger joined them and, noticing their depressed expressions, asked what they were talking about. The two gave a concise version of Jesus' ministry, his crucifixion, the rumor of his empty tomb, and doubt among the disciples. As the three continued on their journey, the stranger explained the Scriptures concerning the Messiah with authority and great knowledge, impressing his traveling companions. When they arrived at Emmaus, the two begged the eloquent stranger to remain with them, an invitation he accepted. Later, over dinner, the guest picked up a piece of bread and said a prayer of thanksgiving, broke the loaf into pieces and passed them to the other two. At that moment, they recognized Jesus. They had walked with him for several hours, heard his voice and listened to him teach, but hadn't known him. Only at the table, in the familiar setting of food and drink, did they recognize their companion as their risen Savior.

Just as the meal at Emmaus changed Jesus' status from religious martyr to resurrected Christ, the Last Supper forever changed the parameters of a meal as the mere consumption of food and discussion of topics. The twelve who celebrated Passover with Jesus feasted on the usual lamb, bread, and wine—newly imbued with meaning. Jesus instructed the disciples to remember the meal's symbolism and eternal significance.

Now, 2000 years later, we gather at the Eucharistic table in remembrance of Jesus. It gives us opportunity to remember the starvation of our soul, the drought of our spirit. We return, again and again, to sit in the presence of the divine, to feast on mysterious love, to be filled with a portion of grace. For some, communion has become little more than a dainty, pious ritual. This is a meal to heartily consume; to devour the bread to satiate our soul's hunger, to gulp the wine as if our very existence depended upon every drop. In the "keeping of the feast," we pray that God will "deliver us from the presumption of coming to the Table for solace only, and not for strength; for pardon only, and not for renewal."[3] It is there we recognize Jesus as our Host and see ourselves, and everyone else, as an unworthy but invited and welcomed guest.

CHAPTER 9

Reflections of Service

❦

As a frequent speaker at women's conferences and retreats, I meet hundreds of women a year. Sometimes while my host attends to other details, I'm left to introduce myself to the arriving women, a courtesy I enjoy. It's always humorous to watch women's expressions when I offer my hand and say, "Hi. I'm Janice Chaffee." When the response of "So?" lifts their eyebrows, I'm quick to add, "The guest speaker." "Oh," they say, faces softening, "it's nice to meet you." Occasionally, my outstretched hand receives only a cool response, which leaves me feeling a bit uneasy.

According to our personalities, we respond differently to meeting strangers. Some of us quickly make new friends, others are more reserved; some are shy and reticent, some bold or self-assured. I've learned that some greetings I've initially perceived as snobbish or icy may only indicate a natural reserve or insecurity.

The first time I heard Gail Hamilton tell her story of meeting a particular group of strangers, I was surprised, even shocked. Without a doubt, it proved that the parables of Jesus accurately capture human nature. My reaction to her experience was all the more acute because Gail is my dear friend and former business partner. But her story taught me that even hurtful introductions can lead to good.

Gail and I co-produced two musical projects, *Sisters* and *Sisters: The Story Goes On,* albums celebrating sisterhood among Christian women. Our partnership was an anomaly to many. When I first met her, Gail was renowned as the producer of several award-winning albums and manager of the very successful vocal group, TAKE 6. She was, and remains, gracefully statuesque with a gentle but undeniable sense of authority. She is calm and deliberate. In contrast, I am a contradictory mix of reserve and exuberance. I am impulsive and vocal. She is African-American and I am Caucasian. We differ in many ways but are as similar as siblings in our longing for personal and spiritual peace, in our adoring devotion to our husbands, passionate love for our children, dedication to our work. There is absolutely no difference in our desire for unity. Consequently, when we produced the albums, we purposefully chose artists of varying styles, races, ages, and denominations to sing the "Sisters" theme song: "No matter how the world defines us, nothing can break the tie that binds us, We are sisters in the Lord."[1]

Shortly after the albums' releases, Gail made one of her frequent business trips to South Africa. The first of several meetings on her schedule was an appointment with her hero, Bishop Desmond Tutu. The two of them had previously met at the Civil Rights Museum in Memphis, Tennessee, where he received the annual Civil Rights Award for his part in the South African struggle for human rights. She had announced the release of a Warner Brothers album titled *March On*. The reason for their meeting in Cape Town was to finalize the Bishop's statement for the album packaging of *Place of Hope,* a project celebrating the "New South Africa."

On a beautiful Friday morning, Gail was thrilled beyond words when Bishop Tutu smiled in recognition and walked across his office to greet her. She was profoundly grateful for the privilege of meeting with him in his own country to discuss civil rights, reconciliation, and especially the future of South Africa's children. She was both giddy and humbled by her private audience with the bishop and with her small role of participating in the reconstruction of South Africa.

The next afternoon, Gail carefully dressed for her appearance at a ladies tea, where, as the guest of honor, she planned to distribute copies of the *Sisters* albums and lead an informal discussion. She was eager to meet South African women and to share her own experiences of Christian sisterhood and the work of racial unity in the United States. Smoothing the front of her mauve dress, she questioned what she would say to this gathering of women, what would make a difference in their lives. *Of course, I'll talk about sisterhood,* she thought, *but spiritual sisterhood requires racial acceptance.* She was curious about South African Christians' stand on apartheid. *But,* she countered herself, *that's not the reason I'm here.* The purpose of this meeting was to provide a safe place for women to freely tell their stories, to admit their differences, to celebrate their similarities, and to strengthen their growing unity. This tea was not a political forum but an occasion to promote sisterhood.

Unexpectedly, Gail was the first to arrive at the tea. She was warmly greeted by her host who promptly scurried off to oversee final preparations. Left alone, Gail wandered over to the linen-covered serving table, set with beautiful china teapots centered on starched doilies between plates of biscuits, scones, and cookies. Tiny silver spoons to stir milk and sugar were set beside cups that would later hold steaming, fragrant teas. Gail was admiring the beauty of the display when the sound of arriving guests caused her to look toward the door. Three or four women entered, chatting easily among themselves.

They approached the table and Gail broadly smiled, excited to meet new friends. She waited for a lull in the conversation to introduce herself. But there was none. Brief smiles flitted between the guest of honor and the women filling their plates with sweets, but no words of welcome. Within a few seconds, more women came through the door and those surrounding the table called out cheery greetings.

But no one spoke to Gail. A bit bewildered, she wondered if they were intentionally ignoring her.

Maybe I gave wrong signals to them, she thought, *or maybe they just didn't notice me.* More women arrived. The Grammy-award-winning producer inhaled and exhaled a calming breath, smiled, and extended her hand to the women walking toward her. One casually draped her sweater across Gail's outstretched arm. No eye contact, no greeting, only an assumption that she was hired help.

Humiliation burned just beneath the surface of her skin—her brown-sugar colored skin. Then it dawned upon her. All the other guests were white. Gail's sudden discomfort with being the only black in a room full of whites was not new, not here in South Africa and not at home. It was a reality she experienced time and time again, always hoping it would be different "next time." But this time wounded her to tears. She was disappointed and sickened by the familiarity of not belonging.

Gail rushed to a side room, closed the door behind her, and dropped onto a couch. The care she had taken to present herself no longer mattered. *God, please don't make me speak to these women today,* she cried. *I can't and I won't.* Hurt turned to extreme sorrow. *I should have stayed in Cape Town, in the company of Bishop Tutu.* The constricting pressure in her throat ached.

Wait, hold on, she cautioned herself. *Maybe it wasn't the color of my skin. Maybe they were uncertain rather than rude.* Gail fought against the assumption that the social snubs of a few were intentional. But she couldn't deny that she was hurt that the women had not acknowledged anything about *her*—not her dress, not her demeanor, not her gesture of friendship.

A knock on the door startled her. Her host's voice called out, "Gail, are you all right? We're ready for you now." It took all her strength to answer, "Okay, I'll be right there."

She lifted herself slowly, trying to still her thoughts, swinging like a pendulum between understanding and anger. She squirmed under a heavy weight of old prejudices and assumptions she felt forced to carry. As her tears fell, the Holy Spirit began a quiet conversation with her soul. In spite of the behavior of her Christian sisters, whether intentional or perceived, she was still bound to them by a common faith.

But they treated me as if I were a servant! she indignantly scoffed. *Good,* came the gentle reply, a rebuttal that cooled her flaring temper. The text of Mark 9:35 came to her mind: "Whoever wants to be first must be last of all and servant of all." *Servant of all.*

Gail's tears of self-pity stopped. She rose from the couch, willing to be a servant of Christ, a servant by choice. More than she wanted the women's acceptance, more than she wanted their attention, she wanted them to hear the message of sisterhood; she wanted them to live in unity beyond boundaries of race and class; she wanted them to build on their history for the sake of the future. She knew she had to begin with her own example.

Gail once more smoothed her dress and walked into the main room, just in time to hear a woman ask, "Well, where's this Gail we've heard so much about?" "Here she is," said the host, gesturing toward Gail, completely unaware of what had taken place earlier. Some women waved in genuine welcome, others called out a softly accented "Hello." A wave of surprise washed over a few faces; their expressions made it clear that they had indeed seen her earlier but had not considered her a guest.

When Gail returned to Nashville and told me this story, my first reaction was typical of me—anger on behalf of my friend. I bristled at the thought of my sister being snubbed when I knew how influential, how respected she was in the music industry. Gail, in her typical fashion, diverted my attention to the end of the story and to the lesson she learned. And as I listened, I was humbled by her willingness to forgive those who, in a figurative sense, seated her at the lowest place at the table. I was convicted by her willingness to serve for the sake of truth.

After her introduction at the tea, Gail sat down and explained the concept for the *Sisters* albums. She described the relationship with her white production partner and their mutual desire for sisterhood. She spoke of her private meeting with Desmond Tutu and their mutual quest for civil rights. At that point, the Holy Spirit halted her monologue. She was saying the right words, but her tone was wrong. Through inflection and carefully chosen words, Gail was forcing those who snubbed her to acknowledge her importance. She was holding them emotionally hostage, just as she was held hostage by her own attitude. Gail lowered her eyes. *I'm sorry,* she prayed. *Help me practice what I preach.* Gail knew that the One she represented was more important than who she was. Her role was to lift up the One who called himself a servant. Gail looked up.

"Let me begin again," she said, "and tell you my personal story." She told them that she had experienced rejection as a child, as a college student, even as an adult. She told them about her divorce, her insecurities, her need for approval. She described her children and her fears as a mother; how her life had been changed by the horrible, accidental death of her daughter's fiancé. She told of her own frightening health battles and the circumstances that brought her to South Africa.

In a new tone, she told them about her partner, Janice, and how they marveled at their similarities and grew comfortable with their differences, how and why the *Sisters* projects were made. "We are sisters by choice," Gail explained, "sisters in our hope and desire for spiritual and racial unity. We have to get along," she smiled, "because we want our children to grow up as brothers and sisters. If we don't model love for them, who will stop the pattern of hate and segregation?"

When she finished, Gail invited each woman to tell her own. Gail listened to homemakers, professional business-women, an actress, an artist, a writer. Each one identified with some aspect of Gail's story and were ready, even eager, for change in their individual lives and in their nation. All the women that day confirmed their desire for a new beginning in a loving, accepting community of sisterhood. The tea concluded with women laughing at their similarities, weeping over their failures, praying for their futures, and committing to unity in Christ.

The hugs Gail received from the women saying their goodbyes greatly contrasted their initial greetings. Between the two experiences, one very important thing had occurred —an honest conversation about reconciliation, the very topic Gail and Bishop Tutu discussed the day before. Someone suggested going to Soweto to help the "needy" blacks in that township. Gail gently suggested that they might begin their work of reconciliation with the black workers in their own homes. Reconciliation, Gail said, cannot begin only with national intent; it must begin as a personal goal with one person, a group of friends, and then spread through one neighborhood, one city, to one county, one country.

How foolish we are to think we might succeed in arranging guests at God's banquet of life. When God arranges the placecards, a prisoner named Nelson Mandela becomes a president, a common fisherman named Peter becomes the leader of the Christian church, a woman directed to the back of a bus and a brave black Baptist preacher change the seating arrangement of an entire nation. When God arranges things, an African-American record executive takes a one-time opportunity to urge white South African women to tell their stories, to join her in sisterhood.

Gail's story reminds us that based on nothing more than a glance, we can form opinions of others, about their significance, about their place. Can you recall a time when you put your purse or coat on the seat of honor to hold it for yourself? Or an instance when that seat was taken away from you or unfairly reserved for another? When we are honest, we admit that we have longed to sit in the important chair.

Jesus knew this about us when he told an unsuspecting group of diners a simple story about a wedding banquet, placecards, and the danger of pride. He knew how ego can drive us forward, how likely we are to elbow our way to prominence. He warns against any false sense of importance or inappropriate ambition. Instead, he knows humility and contentment can be found by taking a lower seat. In God's timing and choosing, we may experience the privilege of being asked to move to a higher seat. This is the paradox of the parable: any place at God's table is honorable if God has assigned it.

The Image
of Grace

Solana: A Loved Daughter

❧

The Departure

The face is the mirror of the mind,
and eyes without speaking confess the secrets of the heart.
—ST. JEROME, 342–420

The awful thing is that beauty is mysterious
as well as terrible.
God and devil are fighting there,
and the battlefield is the heart of man.
—FYODOR MIKHAILOVICH DOSTOEVSKI, 1821–1881

Solana ran her tongue over the gummy film coating her teeth, then rolled her head away from reeking drool on the pillowcase. She squinted against the morning glare and tried to sit up, but fell back as the walls seemed to warp and buckle. She clenched her jaws to hold down whirlpooling nausea, a vile party favor from last night's snow-covered tequila shooters. Her hangover pounded as loudly as last night's mariachi band. Pulling the covers over her head, she silently groaned, *I hate my life and this horrible family I'm stuck in.*

Lying perfectly still between soft sheets, Solana sulked and plotted. *I have to get out of here, and with my fair share. I deserve it.* The thought swelled like an obstinate mantra. The *señorita* was accustomed to getting her own way, and today would be no exception. She had learned at an early age that beauty was often entitlement to privilege and indulgence. Conceit was the conduit to her every whim and desire being granted. And what she wanted was out—out of this house and family.

This is the day. Solana kicked off the sheet, slid her feet into wool slippers, and pulled on a lavender silk robe. She froze for a moment to still the painful sloshing in her head. "Papa!" she bellowed as she stumbled downstairs. As expected, her father was in the kitchen eating Dolorea's homemade tortillas with scrambled eggs. The greasy smell of frying chorizos nearly made her gag.

She swallowed hard, then blurted, "Papa, I want to leave home. You're already old and don't need all your money so just give me my inheritance now. I want control of my own life." The virulence of Solana's voice and breath widened her father's eyes and stopped his fork midair. Dolorea, who had helped raise this girl from infancy, was stunned by this new level of insolence. "Well, good morning, *mi hija,* my daughter," said her father. "Surprised to see you up so early. Would you like something to eat to celebrate this special occasion?" As usual, he attempted humor to calm his impetuous child.

"Oh, Papa, you *never* take me seriously." She plopped into a chair, pouting like a baby. Dolorea quietly set a glass of orange juice before her. Solana glanced up at their house-keeper-cook, the only mother figure she and her sister Constancia had known.

"Gracias," she said after draining the whole glass. The juice was a sweet relief to her dry mouth. Solana watched her father chewing, his weathered skin contracting like old leather bellows. Her gaze traced the contours and wrinkles of age and responsibility. Nearly everyone in the entire town worked for him, it seemed. Everyone but Solana. Her older sister loved the family business, but she didn't. And never would. She tugged her fingers through the tangles of her dark wavy hair and thought, *I'd rather die than be like Connie.* The very idea sent a shiver down her spine.

She narrowed her eyes against the brightness of the kitchen and mentally confirmed her reasons to leave. *Nothing ever changes in this boring place. I'm sick of the friends I've known since kindergarten. All the dorky girls get married and play house with fat babies, and all the boys settle for predicable jobs.* Contempt blew out between her vain lips. *No one understands me.*

"Papa, there's nothing for me here," she insisted. "What am I supposed to do? Live in town and work for you?" An indignant snort punctuated her questions. "I want a different life, a *fun* life. I want to meet people who talk about more than last week's weather, tomorrow's auction, or yesterday's soap opera. I want out of here, Papa," she pleaded. "I'm grown up, so *por favor,* please, let me go."

His daughter's puffy, bloodshot eyes perverted her smooth young face. *Mi bebé, my baby,* he thought, *my naive, headstrong girl.* For months he had sensed this confrontation coming, and now, here she was, hungover and demanding emancipation. She was asking, but her defiant tone let him know that his ability to restrain her had come to an end. Her heart was already gone. "Are you sure that's what you want?" he asked.

Solana blinked uncomfortably. She hated when he looked at her like that, as if he could see her secrets. Gazing back into eyes as dark as her own, she saw her father's love. She squirmed under his piercing gaze.

"Yes, it really is what I want! I'll be okay," she promised. "I just want out of here so I can go live my own life." She turned her head to cough, her lungs congested and craving a cigarette.

I know your life, he thought. *I know about the drugs and drinking and the all-night raves; the sleeping around, the sneaking and lying. I know that you don't control your choices, but your choices control you.* It appalled him that despite his guidance, his beloved daughter somehow believed that sex was love, popularity meant respect, and that rebellion expressed individualism. He slowly said, "Your share of the estate will be quite substantial, Solana. Are you sure you can handle the responsibility of that much money?"

"You see! That's what I mean," Solana cried out. "No matter what I say, you make me feel stupid. You're always right and I'm always wrong; you're always the adult and I'm always the dumb little kid." Her frustration grew like a spiraling dust devil. "I hate living here," she shrieked. "I hate your rules and restrictions and going to that stupid mission and listening to all that—" She knew not to say her favorite phrase, not in front of her father. But she abhorred Sunday mass. Sermons had the same mind-numbing effect as a history class or the nature channel. The homily was wasted prattle about myths she didn't believe.

She pulled her hair with both hands. *How did I wind up talking about church?* She took a breath and started again. "I know you hate my friends. And all you do is criticize my clothes and my hair and my music. You don't understand me at all!"

Her father was thinking the same thing. *You don't understand me, my beloved girl.* He quietly spoke. "I don't hate your friends, Solana. Admittedly, I don't approve of the ones who take advantage of you. Your clothes and your music aren't the problem, honey. I don't care if you have a shaved head and a zillion earrings or if you wear weird clothes. What I worry about is what you do to yourself, your hostile attitude, your deceit and defiance…"

"You twist my words like balloon animals!" she sobbed. "I want to talk about leaving, and you're sending me on a guilt trip." Her face reddened with rage.

And you can't hear what I'm saying over your desire to do what you want, thought her father. *You think that just by wanting something, you should have it. Mi hija, you'll still be you when you leave, and you'll never find what you're looking for, because it doesn't exist. There's no such thing as life without responsibilities, choices without consequences.* It seemed to him that attention was her most addictive drug. He wished his own love and acceptance were enough to satisfy her neediness, but they weren't. She wanted recognition, but not from him. This truth made him wince with parental sorrow.

"Solana, contrary to what you think, I don't want you to remain a child forever," he said. "You'll be a great woman if you develop your gifts and properly use the privileges you've been given." He paused, reluctant to speak the consensual words. "So, if you insist on your independence, I'll go to the bank today and open an account in your name. I'll arrange for your portion of the estate to be under your control."

Solana couldn't believe it was over that easily. She had expected a much longer fight. She jumped up with a whoop and hugged her father. "*Gracias,* Papa," she shouted. "This is so great!" She leaned against his muscular, warm chest, more to regain her balance than show gratefulness.

Constancia rolled her eyes in response to her spoiled little sister's squeal. She had overheard their entire conversation, hidden behind the arched entry to the kitchen. *Another moment of live theater,* she smirked; *the drama queen's latest performance.*

Solana nearly knocked over her sister as she bolted from the room shouting, "I'm out of here!" A smile stretched out Connie's lips. *That's the best news I've ever heard,* she gloated. *I'm finally rid of that brat!* Her hateful thoughts dissipated at the sound of their father clearing his throat. There was no way he would share her elation, so she tiptoed to the front door and quietly let herself out, off to work, well away from the theatrics of her sister and acquiescence of her father.

The girls' father sat at the kitchen table, miserable and damp-eyed. "I have to let Solana go," he admitted to Dolorea. "She is old enough to make her own decisions, even if I don't agree with them." His wide, strong hands lay limp on the table in acknowledgment of what he had just granted. The very thought of *su niñita,* his little girl, leaving home for an almost predictable future grieved him to the bone. *Ay, mi corazón se está rompiendo,* he silently wept. *Oh, my breaking heart.*

Solana spent the next few days sorting, folding, and packing, hesitating only once in her manic task. Lifting an ornately carved jewelry box inlaid with lapis, she called out, "Papa, is it okay if I take the pearl necklace and diamond earrings?"

"Of course," he assured her, "those were my gifts to you." Solana didn't notice the sadness shading her father's voice, the melancholy drifting through the house.

On the day of her departure, Solana woke early, her stomach taut with excitement. After she showered, dressed, and made a final appraisal in the mirror, she ran down the stairs. She found Dolorea in the kitchen, scouring spotless counters, and mumbled an aloof goodbye. Her sister had already left on a deliberately scheduled business trip to avoid the wildest of her sister's attention-getting schemes.

Solana leapt into the truck where her father waited. "Let's go, Papa." Neither one turned on the radio, so they rode in silence all the way to the airport. Her father ached to say something, to beg his daughter to stay, to advise her to be careful, to wish her well, but all that had already been said. Solana was grateful for the silence; she didn't want to argue and didn't want to hear any reason to doubt her decision to leave.

At the airport terminal, Solana nervously flittered around her suitcases, getting in the way of skycaps tagging each bag. Waiting at the gate, she tapped her boarding pass against her leg and shifted from foot to foot until the call to board finally came over the loudspeakers. Trembling with impatience, she quickly embraced her father. He wanted to hold her forever, but let her go.

"*Adiós,* Papa," she said. "Don't worry. I promise to keep in touch." She laughed at his somber expression and said, "Ease up, I'll be fine!"

He whispered, "Be safe, *mi hija.* Don't ever forget that I love you." But Solana wasn't listening. She was already running up the jetway to the plane. Had she looked back, she would have seen her father, bent and murmuring, "*Adiós, mi hija bella. Qué Dios te guarde.* God keep you safe."

The Arrival

The human understanding is like a false mirror,
which, receiving rays irregularly,
distorts and discolors the nature of things
by mingling its own nature with it.
—FRANCIS BACON, 1561–1626

Oft expectation fails, and most oft there
Where most it promises.
—WILLIAM SHAKESPEARE, 1564–1616

Solana lifted her face up to the blazing sun. She breathed in the scent of the city and exhaled all lingering doubts of whether she should have moved to Dallas. Her father, true to his word, had put her share of the inheritance into an account. Amazement rather than gratitude overwhelmed her when she saw the sequence of commas and zeros in the opening balance of her financial statement. *This will last a lifetime,* she thought.

Her first shopping excursion to Turtle Creek made Solana feel like Miss Backwater, self-conscious in clothes that now itched with homespun dowdiness. Insecurity and tenacity accompanied her through the doors of a famous boutique. For years she had admired this designer's ads in fashion magazines. Wandering between chrome fixtures reflecting halogen pinspots, Solana hesitantly fingered size-four samples draped on surreal mannequins. A tall, thin blonde approached and snipped, "May I help you?" Solana couldn't tell if the accent was affected by locale or snobbery.

"Oh, sure...I, um, need some new clothes," Solana stumbled. "Really?" the clerk replied. Solana's cheeks burned with embarrassment. There was no mistaking the insinuation. "And just *what* kind of clothes do you need?"

Solana faltered. "Well, for the theater and dinner and. . ." The blonde's charcoal-lined eyes rolled over Solana as if assessing her worth. "Are you limited to a price range?" she asked. Solana opened her wallet to reveal a metallic rainbow of credit cards. "Not with these," she said a little too eagerly. "There's no limit."

Hours later, Solana's new Jaguar convertible was filled with boxes and bags stuffed with an entirely new wardrobe. After carrying out the last load, Lucinda apologized for her initial rudeness. "It's so tedious to wait on women who have no intention of buying," she explained, "tourists who waste my time trying on clothes they can't afford. Since you're new in town," Lucinda added as a gesture of reparation, "why don't you join me and a friend for dinner tonight?" Solana laughed with relief and hugged her newfound friend. "I'd love to," she said.

Back in her hotel suite, Solana tried on every new outfit, hardly able to decide what to wear to dinner, finally slipping into a thousand dollars worth of black silk. She twirled in front of the mirror, a proud smile complementing her transformation. *This is it,* Solana thought. *I'm finally where I belong! And no one to keep me from having fun!*

Lucinda waited outside one of the city's finest restaurants, and next to her stood the most gorgeous male Solana had ever seen. After a quick embrace, Lucinda said, "Solana, I'd like you to meet Rush." The fashionably-dressed man laughed at the newcomer's inability to speak. "Nice to meet you, too," he replied in a voice as sensuous as a warm island wind. "Let's go inside and have a drink!"

Seated in a burgundy leather banquette, the trio's laughter blended like well-tuned chimes. Lucinda and Rush were exactly the people Solana expected to find in Dallas. When the waiter appeared with a tray of drinks and appetizers, Solana smiled, imagining the shocked expressions of people back home. *If they could see me now,* she thought, *with a martini in one hand, a cigar in the other.* Impervious to their certain criticism, she lifted her glass to toast the sophistication of friends she had wanted all her life to meet.

Her first gourmet experience in Dallas exceeded her wildest dreams. Solana insisted on paying for dinner and turned a deaf ear to her friends' protests. She slid a platinum card inside the leather check presenter while Lucinda and Rush shrugged in resignation. Solana added a $200 tip, signed the tab with exaggerated flair, unaware that the future had been set. The three left the restaurant and headed off to a series of clubs.

Solana stared with disbelief at the red numbers on the clock. She had slept for…how long? Leaving the last club the night before and getting back to her hotel weren't exactly clear in her memory. She looked down at her new dress, twisted around her body like a ribbon on a Maypole.

After a few hours of intermittent dozing, Solana woke enough to realize she was craving Dolorea's soup. Most of her childhood ailments had been cured with homemade albondagas. She wondered if even that remedy would ease her present misery, then rolled over and went back to sleep.

Solana rarely thought of home. She had discarded her former identity as easily as her old wardrobe. With deliberate attention, she managed to sound like a stylish Texan. She rid herself of all that hinted of anything but a born-and-bred society girl. Her past was remembered as a girl she used to know, blurred by time, separated by experience. The only link between her small-town past and the big-city present was the quest for admiration.

Months and seasons passed like time-lapse photography. Solana immersed herself in the city that roiled with action. As promised, Rush and Lucinda introduced her to a fast crowd and a frenetic schedule. Sunday mornings summoned sleep, not worship. Religious traditions of her youth were stored away, along with the memory of those people who imposed their rigid morals and archaic values on her. She knew she was drinking too much, sleeping too little and much too carelessly, but flattery and increasing popularity was the antidote.

Texas wildflowers bloomed and then withered under the scorching sun. Thunder rattled above the plains, lightning flared in the sky, but Solana paid no attention to nature or the elements. She was preoccupied with her independent and intoxicating pursuit of pleasure. On an overcast morning, Solana woke up with the vague recollection of a large table surrounded by rowdy people. Her now-customary hangover made the ring of the telephone sound like a stuttering jackhammer. The hotel business officer identified himself and then crisply announced that her credit limit had been exceeded. "How can that be?" she asked.

"When did you make your last payment?" he asked.

Astonished silence absorbed both ends of the line. "I think you should call your bank," was the clerk's clipped response. Solana grimaced at the sound of the receiver crashing into its cradle and then got out of bed to search for the bottle of pain relievers.

She sank into a soft leather chair in a bank manager's office. The persistent throbbing in her head made it nearly impossible to follow the man's nasal droning. His precise vocabulary reminded her of her Papa blathering some nonsense about getting what you buy or paying for what you get. The manager cleared his throat to recapture her attention. "Look," he said, "you're in a bit of a jam here, but I can help. Don't worry, we'll get all this straightened out. For a small fee, I'll personally manage your account. Continue to make all of your purchases on credit cards, but have the bills sent to me. When you need cash, come in and I'll be happy to serve you. Just watch your spending since you've already made significant withdrawals from your fund."

Solana was relieved. Who wanted to waste time making payments, balancing statements, keeping track of receipts? The banker's emphasis on his small fee and her significantly reduced balance flew right over her pretty little head.

≈ ≈ ≈

"Come on, it will be fun. We'll have a blast as roommates," Lucinda insisted. "I can't believe you've lived in a hotel suite for so long, no matter how plush it is!" Lucinda's voice was convincing. So Solana rented a spacious loft and the two friends spent weeks buying sofas, chairs, rugs, and every accessory their hearts desired. Stocking the kitchen was last as neither one knew how to cook. The hand-painted china and the copper pans were more for decoration than function. *This* is *fun,* Solana admitted. *My own place in my own style.* She seemed unfazed by the fact that Lucinda contributed a great deal of her opinion but very little cash.

The passage of time was noticed only by the changes in Solana's wardrobe. She thrived on shopping, new restaurants, movies, plays, and art gallery openings, rejuvenated by seasonal trips to the beach or slopes. A great deal of money and effort were necessary to maintain an "It girl" reputation and run with an ever-growing entourage. Her thoughts pivoted around the next social entry in her calendar; she thought of little else. The next event, she decided, would be a night out with her current boyfriend.

She picked up the phone and called Marcus. "Hey, Hon," she said when he answered, "what are you doing?"

"I was just thinking about taking you away for the weekend," he said. "Want to go down to the coast for a couple of days?"

"The coast? I'd love it! I'll be packed in 20 minutes," she gushed. "I'll fill up the Jag, then pick you up." She hummed a little song as she threw a bikini and a couple of sexy dresses in a suitcase. *This is just what I need,* she thought, *a wonderful weekend with Marcus.*

It was wonderful. They brunched on lox, bagels, and caviar and the finest bottles of champagne. Every night they danced until the band went home, then called room service for a three A.M. feast. Solana hated to leave when they repacked on Monday. There was a slight delay at the checkout desk, when the registrar professionally and quietly informed Marcus that his credit card had been denied. Marcus flashed his perfect smile at Solana and said, "Sorry, Baby, I guess my payment didn't get there in time." "That's okay," she said, and reached for her wallet. Marcus took the valet ticket for the Jag to the door while Solana paid.

The clerk slid the receipt across the marble counter for Solana to sign. As she handed the pen back she was intrigued by the inquisitive look on his face. "Yes?" she asked. He averted his eyes, then looked back at Solana. "Forgive me for imposing," he hesitated. "But really, you shouldn't let yourself be treated like this. You aren't the first young lady to bail out this guy at this hotel. You deserve better." Solana stared at him and couldn't decide whether to say "Drop dead" or "Thank you."

Lucinda seldom spent the night in the loft, but evidence of her existence piled on the tables, bunched up in the corners, and stained the furniture. *Enough of this,* Solana fumed. *Lucinda has to move out.* When the sloppy roommate finally returned a few nights later, she brought Rush and a somewhat recognizable group with her. "Look what we have," shouted Lucinda at the top of her voice. "A party!" Someone cranked up the CD player while others unloaded grocery bags filled with liquors, mixers, and snacks. The coffee table was cleared to make room for an abundance of drugs and paraphernalia. Solana forgot all about evicting Lucinda.

The next day's sun was on its descent when tinny music irritated Solana into consciousness. Her muddled mind recognized the cartoon theme song. *Why is the TV on, and why is it so freakin' loud?* she wondered. She groped for the remote control, opened her eyes, and looked for the volume button. Then she noticed the disaster in her room. Splayed closet doors framed empty hangers dangling from the metal rod; only a sweater and pair of jeans hung lopsided and forsaken. The jewelry chest was tipped on its side, drawers askew and empty. She propped herself up on one elbow to see never-worn clothes and designer shoes scattered on the floor as if they had played a game of Freeze while she slept.

Solana couldn't imagine what had happened. She lifted her arm to toss back the covers, then winced in pain. She hobbled across the bedroom, opened the door and peered into the living area. She saw nothing. Literally, nothing. Gone were the chairs, the sofa, the coffee table, the large Persian rug; gone were the television, stereo, CD player, and speakers. Original art had been stripped from walls, pedestals left barren. Crumpled chip bags, crushed soda cans, empty liquor bottles, and overflowing ashtrays were all that remained on the bare oak floor.

Suddenly weak, Solana staggered to the bathroom and screamed. She reeled at the reflection of a badly battered face; eyes ringed in dull black, bruised cheeks, welted neck. An uncomprehending cry escaped swollen, split lips. *Oh, God. Oh, God, what has happened to me?* tore through her mind. Horrified that she had no memory of an obvious attack, she collapsed to the floor. Only then did she see brownish, dried blood streaking her legs. What Solana couldn't remember, she knew.

She crawled to the shower stall and pulled herself in. Near-scalding water pelted her ravaged body. Steam swirled around her like vapors of guilt. On the verge of hysteria, she shampooed her hair twice and repeatedly soaped her skin. Only her soul remained out of reach from her maniacal scrubbing.

For days, the lights were kept off and the curtains drawn. Curled between the sheets, Solana furiously planned revenge and recovery. *I'll survive this,* she adamantly swore. *I'll make new friends. I'll do whatever it takes to get a job and live a better life.* Beauty was still her passport to success, and her determination to reach it was more voracious than ever.

For the first time in her life, Solana didn't get exactly what she wanted when she wanted it. No experience and no employment history equaled no job. Once or twice, she dropped her father's name as a reference, but no one cared who he was or what he owned in wherever it was he lived. And it was fruitless trying to regain anything that had been stolen. None of it was insured and she hadn't kept any receipts. Lucinda and Rush had apparently given her false last names. Their cell phone service had been disconnected and both had quit their last jobs without leaving forwarding addresses. Her only sense of comfort was in the fact that they hadn't found the pearls and diamonds from her father. For some unknown reason, months earlier, she had decided to hide them in a fake book.

The emptiness of the loft was depressing. She was afraid to stay in a place with such violent memories, so she moved to a smaller, cheaper apartment. Solana was convinced her luck would change, but her habits had not. She spent money on trendy furnishings and the same sort of friends—flashy and fast, human leeches attached to Solana's foolish spending.

On her way back from yet another pointless job interview, Solana passed the restaurant she first ate in with Lucinda and Rush. In the autumn twilight, she stopped and watched well-dressed pedestrians hurrying to their destinations, oblivious of one other. *We're all bunched up together, but so alone,* she wistfully observed. A Bentley backing into a parking space just across the street caught her eye. A stylish couple climbed out. Lucinda first, followed by Rush, who turned to offer his hand to a lovely young woman, a beautiful girl, so fresh, so innocent, so much a blonde version of herself. They were entranced by their new friend. In a blinding flash of clarity, Solana saw the scam. *Well, let the little hayseed learn the hard way,* she thought without an ounce of compassion. *Welcome to the city, Darlin'. Ya'll have a real good time.*

≈ ≈ ≈

Ignoring the inevitable became a fine art. Reality set in when Solana attempted to buy a cashmere sweater for the mild winter. Not a single credit card in her wallet accepted the charge. Livid and insulted, she pushed through the crowded sidewalks on the way to the bank. She cared not at all what people thought of her; she thought nothing of them. Storming past the corral of blue velvet ropes, she bolted straight to the counter, demanding to speak with her personal manager. The polite revelation, "He no longer works here," paralyzed her like a poisonous dart. Solana's lips stuck to her teeth as she asked to see a statement of her account. The teller returned with the impossible. "I'm sorry, ma'am, that account was closed due to insufficient funds."

Fear curdled her stomach. In just a few years, she had blown her entire inheritance. She lunged for a nearby wastebasket and violently retched. The clerk's mouth moved but Solana heard nothing. Staggering back to her apartment, she formulated a plan. *I have $500 cash in my wallet. I'll take some of my clothes to a consignment shop,* she thought. *I'll move to an even cheaper place. I'll get work, any kind of work. There are plenty of people in this town hiring beautiful women.*

As it had before, packing strengthened her resolve. *It's about time I finally took charge of my life,* she muttered under her breath. Opening the fake book, she caressed the lustrous pearls and shimmering diamonds. *I'll never sell these,* she promised herself. Haughtiness clasped the strand around her neck and fastened the posts in her ears.

Day after day, week after week, the only financially substantial offers came with a licentious sneer and the dangle of a hotel room key. *Why not?* she shrugged. *What was stolen from me, I can sell. I'll be just like Julia Roberts in* Pretty Woman—*particular about my clients. I want money and there's no quicker way to earn it.* It hardly mattered when the green bills morphed into white dust and small crystal rocks in tiny glass vials. Seasons came and went without notice, without a wardrobe change.

Where am I? It took a few more minutes before the peeling plaster walls of the crack house came into focus. Sunlight slipped in around the edges of cardboard tacked over the windows. She had no clue of the time, day, or even the month. The stench of urine burned her nose. Sharp pains clawed her stomach. *Where am I?*

In that moment, truth ambushed Solana. She was lost in a barren maze of nowhere. She had no friends, no money, no car. There was no fame, no dream come true. Nothing mattered, not her life, not her body. *But I'm still me,* she defiantly lifted her chin. Instinctively she raised her hand to her neck, then ears. The pearl necklace and diamond earrings were gone. Filth and shame were her only adornments. It took every ounce of willpower for her to look at her surroundings. Faintly visible in the dusty light, snoring strangers reminded her of pigs sleeping by the neighbor's barn back home. *Only,* she thought, *the pigs had been contented, not drugged.*

In her stillness, she remembered having once slept on clean sheets in a home where she was dearly loved. As her head cleared, she made no effort to move. *I refused to work in my Papa's company because it was beneath me. Now the only thing beneath me is a fetid floor in rat-infested room.* The irony did not escape her.

For the first time in years, Solana let herself linger over thoughts of home, of Papa, of Dolorea. *I wasn't very kind when I said goodbye to Dolorea,* she recalled. *What an odd thing to remember after all these years.* She stared at her trembling hands and thought of Connie. They both had inherited their father's long, tapered fingers.

Her only option was to get up. Get up and go home. Her father's seasonal workers were better off than this. They worked for minimum wage but had plenty of food and safe housing. Her father made sure of that. *If I go home,* she thought, *maybe Papa will hire me.* She had disgraced herself too thoroughly to expect more than an entry-level position running errands or cleaning equipment, but she would do anything to get out of this hellhole.

Solana put a hand on the rough boards to push herself up and felt the edge of her little evening bag. Her heart pounded as she pulled the purse from beneath her leg and pressed open the tarnished clasp. Empty. Not a comb, not even a lipstick. She closed her eyes and dropped her head, too depleted to cry. Long-suppressed memories shot across her mind: velvet purses and matching dresses, a full tummy and flannel pajamas, two little girls standing in front of a father teaching them how to prepare for emergencies. Solana remembered. She released the clasp again and pulled on an inconspicuous thread. She slowly lifted a hundred dollar bill from behind the lining. It was enough for a bus ticket home. And a pair of cheap sandals.

Heads turned as the flapping of Solana's rubber flip-flops echoed in the bus depot. Mothers wondered where the dirty, homeless woman was going. Children wondered why she was shaking so badly. Men could tell what she once had been but was no longer—beautiful. Solana thought of her one hope—home.

The Return

Pride goeth before, and shame cometh behind.
—TREATISE OF A GALLANT, C. 1510

How like the prodigal doth she return,
With over-weathered ribs and ragged sails,
Lean, rent, and beggared by the strumpet wind!
—WILLIAM SHAKESPEARE, 1564–1616

Scrunched in a blue plaid bus seat, Solana rehearsed a speech for an audience of one. *Papa, I was wrong. I'm not even worthy to be called tu hija, your daughter. Please give me a job. I'll do anything you want me to do. Papa, Lo siento mucho…I'm so sorry…"*

Mile after mile, across flat, scorched deserts, across invisible borders and time zones, she visualized her father stiffly towering above her, arms crossed, scowling in anger. She knew he loved her once, but she couldn't assume his love now. "Fine," was the answer she imagined. "You can work for an hourly wage with no benefits. But don't expect anything else from me." Solana could live with that.

The crumbling ceiling tiles and cracked linoleum squares of her hometown bus terminal offered a dingy welcome. She wondered if she had made a terrible mistake by returning. Her eyes darted around the station, half expecting a chorus of neighbors to jump out and condemn in unison, "We knew you'd come crawling back. You weren't such a hotshot after all, were you?" She hurried out the door and slunk down familiar streets. On the outskirts of town, miles from her father's estate, Solana faltered. The quiet was unsettling in contrast to the wail of the city. Dizzy with doubt, she stared at the ground, jittery from withdrawal. She inched along. Dirt coated her feet, every slap of her sandals hit like a reproach. Step-by-step, phrase-by-phrase, she recited the speech she had prepared for her father.

The red-tiled roof of her childhood home had just come into view when an odd noise caused Solana to stop. She shielded her eyes from the sun's glare with quivering hands and searched for the source. Dread gripped her heart as a mirage-like form shimmered ahead. She squinted at the wavy silhouette centered in an ethereal cloud of dust. The approaching sound swelled to a chant-like rhythm. She stretched her neck forward to hear the familiar lilt, then gasped as sound slid into words. *No! It can't be!* Confusion and bewilderment constricted her chest. Someone was calling her name. *Solana! Solana! Solana!* She fell to her knees, overwhelmed by the sight of a man running at full speed, arms and legs wildly pumping. *Oh, could it be?* Uncontrollable sobs burst from her aching lungs as she collapsed on an earthen rug of shame. She hid her face in her hands and chanted her own litany: *Papa, Papa, Papa.*

Solana's father pulled his beloved girl up in his arms. His embrace smothered his daughter as she choked out her remorse. *"Papa, Lo siento mucho.* I'm not even worthy to be called *tu hija…"*

That's all she could say. Her father was laughing and crying so hard he wasn't listening to a word. He swooped her up like she was a little girl and kissed her hair and eyelashes. Over and over he whispered, *"Mi bebé bella,"* and practically carried her the rest of the way home.

"Dolorea! *Mi niñita ha regresado!* My little girl is home!" shouted the ecstatic father bursting into the kitchen. Solana stood on wobbly feet, enduring another round of hugs and laughter and tears. Dolorea cooed in Spanish while her husband Manuel squeezed his hat in one hand and wiped his eyes with the other. But Papa—her papa was over the top, laughing and crying, hugging and beaming.

"Let's have a party! Invite everyone to come over tomorrow to celebrate my Solana's return! No, make it Saturday so we have time to make it the best party ever!" His eyes shone upon his daughter's face. Addressing no one in particular, he said, "It's like she was lost out in the world and now she's found her way back! I was so afraid I'd never see her again, but here she is—alive! Home!"

His deep voice cracked with emotion. "Dolorea, call in all the help you need to whip up a feast. Make all your special desserts! Manuel, get Carlos and Joe to butcher a calf and get it on the spit. Tell Paulo and his crew to pick whatever's ripe in the garden. What a party this is going to be!" His smile radiated pure love. Solana turned her face away, realizing that no one in Dallas had ever looked at her that way.

"*Bebé,* you must be tired," he observed. "After you eat something, run upstairs for a long hot bath, then crawl into bed for a while. And Sweetness," he blinked a little sheepishly, "as soon as you feel like it, go shopping. Make sure you get a party dress for Saturday night. Buy anything you want— new shoes, dresses, robes, whatever you need. *Bebé,* I'm so glad you're home." Without taking his eyes from her face, he took her dry, rough hand in his and slipped a ring on her finger. A flawless pearl shimmered against her dirty, cracked skin. Solana blushed as pictures of her past flashed on her screen of guilt: exchanging her father's love for money, abandoning her heritage, wasting her inheritance and her beauty. The doting father reached out and lifted her chin. "I've been saving this for you. All is forgiven and forgotten, *mi princesa,* my princess. Welcome home."

Solana lay motionless in rose-scented bath water, subdued with exhaustion, watching the tiny rainbows curve on clear bubbles, the rolling steam frost the windows. She mentally replayed the events of the last hours, weighing her expectation against the reality. *How wrong I was about Papa. Why did I doubt for a minute that he would be glad to see me?*

Waterlogged and clean, she climbed out of the tub, wound one towel around her thin body and another around her scraggly wet hair. Easing onto the dressing table stool, Solana was startled by her reflection in the mirror. In Dallas mirrors, she saw the illusion of beauty. Here, every line, every vein, every failure was visible. Deep crow's feet chiseled by neglect framed her eyes. The naked truth of a once-pretty girl worn old by deception and vanity was stark. Then, she caught a glimpse of something she had never noticed. She looked like her father.

The next morning, Solana prowled through her father's closet, searching for something she remembered from childhood. She smiled as she put on his old striped robe, the one lined with white terry cloth. It was soft and comfortable and smelled of his aftershave. She wrapped it around her then went downstairs to the kitchen. She laughed at the flurry of activity, the organized chaos. Her sense of happiness surprised her. It had been such a long time since she laughed without cynicism. The familiar aromas of Dolorea's spices, the colorful bouquets of fresh flowers, the authority of her father's voice brought her comfort and security. Even with all the busyness, calm permeated the house. Solana was overwhelmed by everyone's kindness and love. Well, nearly everyone's.

The Reunion

Speech is a mirror of the soul:
as a man speaks, so is he.
—PUBLILIUS SYRUS, FIRST CENTURY B.C.

And lovelier things have mercy shown
To every failing but their own;
And every woe a tear can claim,
Except an erring sister's shame.
—GEORGE NOEL GORDON, LORD BYRON, 1787–1874

Connie was tired at the end of another long week out on the road, visiting clients, playing the corporate game, representing the company. One look at her desk and she immediately knew it had been a mistake to stop at the office instead of going straight home from the airport. She fell into her chair and flipped through stacks of files. She keyed in her password on the computer and wearily scrolled down the long list of e-mails waiting to be read. *Not now,* she sighed to herself. *I'm going home.*

She pushed on her yellow Porsche's accelerator. It had been a long time since she had enjoyed a night of peace and quiet at home. *My home.* A smug smile eased the tension around her mouth as she passed the barns, the livestock, the processing plants, the fields, the staff housing. *They're all mine.* She had worked hard to follow in her father's footsteps. She knew clients initially regarded her as a "Papa's Girl," but she never let her exasperation show when a meeting ended with a pat on the back and the instruction, "Have your old man give me a call and we'll finish up. How's he doing these days?" It took years of fake smiles and firm handshakes to finally establish her authority. Sometimes it seemed her biggest job was not to keep the company going at peak performance but to maintain her father's stellar reputation. She knew the employees secretly talked about the glory days with her father at the helm. But she was tough on them for a reason: to keep a standard worthy of his pride. She expected no more from them than she expected of herself: total devotion.

Zooming down the tree-lined country lane that led to the stucco house, her eyes contracted in the strobe-like bursts of light and shadow. *How like my life,* she observed. *In the limelight, in my father's shadow.* Even though she now ran the business, she often felt like a little girl when he asked, "What did you do today, dear?" His theoretical retirement did nothing to diminish his daily scrutiny. Some days she felt like a puppet tied to strings of parental obligation.

She slammed the accelerator to the floor, her foot weighted with impatience. Nothing went fast enough to suit her. Incompetence infuriated her. She couldn't quite identify her general malaise. She shifted into overdrive, the wind tunnel isolating her thoughts. *What's the point of all this, anyway? Where's the satisfaction? Happiness? Ha! What a stupid sentiment.* She was a beautiful, admired, and pampered member of an elite group, recognized by her prominent name. *I am my father's daughter.* It always came back to that. *My father's daughter.* A blessing and a curse.

This rare session of musings ended at the entrance of the long driveway leading to the house. Connie turned down the blaring golden-oldies CD, shifted into neutral and waited for a parade of trucks to pass. They rolled out one after the other like an automated trail of ants. Baffled, she tapped her foot on the brake and read company logos painted on the side of each exiting van: FedEx, Blooms n' Flowers, Hand and Foot Pampering (Manicures and Pedicures at Home), Lawn Party Rentals. *Why in the world were these trucks at her house?* she wondered.

When the last van made its turn, Connie shifted into first and sped up the driveway. The circular loop in front of the house looked like a used car lot, crammed with vehicles parked half on the lawn and half on the asphalt. Some she identified as belonging to the priest, the owner of the local newspaper, the town mayor, her company officers, and even members of her board of directors.

Good grief. The garage doors were blocked, an irritating inconvenience. *What are all these people doing here?* she fumed.

She opened the car door, when, as if on cue, the simultaneous thrashing of guitar strings and the low tremor of a bass shook the ground. The screech of an ascending trumpet scale split the air. Obviously a band was tuning up. But why? Suspicion knotted her stomach. *This is not good,* she thought.

There was no way she was going through the front door without knowing what was going on. Once again, her father hadn't bothered to tell her that he was hosting another one of his stupid events. *When is this going to end? He never tells me what he's planning. Is this one of his spontaneous get-togethers?* She briskly headed toward a side delivery entrance. A UPS driver bolted out of the house and jogged toward his van.

"Hey!" Connie shouted. "What's going on here?"

The man in brown shrugged. "I heard the old man's missing daughter is back, and he's throwing a big welcome-home bash."

Veins throbbed in her neck and her cheeks flushed with rage. Her chest heaved. *Oh, my God! She's here!* Connie pressed red acrylic nails into her palms. *Why didn't she stay away, why did she have to come home? This is my worst nightmare come true. I prayed this day would never come.* She panicked. *Leave, I've got to leave. No one saw me drive up, so I'll just take off.*

But it wasn't going to be that easy. Her father came running toward her from the front lawn.

"Connie, Connie, guess what?" he grinned like a kid at Christmas. "You won't believe what's happened!"

Oh, but she would. She refused to be trapped in this game of Guess Who's Papa's Favorite and chose her words deliberately. "Let me guess. That whore daughter of yours has returned?"

His jaw fell in disbelief.

She savored his shock. This was her opportunity to tell him everything she hadn't said before. Emotions that had been shoved down for years rushed for release. It was now or never.

"You know what?" she snarled. "I am the oldest, and I've always done exactly what was expected of me. I was the good girl; I finished college and went straight to work in your company. Forget about getting married and having babies; they weren't on my agenda. I climbed your corporate ladder from the mailroom up. 'It's good experience to start at the bottom,' you claimed. Well, it wasn't experience, it was humiliating. The owner's daughter stuck in the stinking mailroom.

But I worked hard. I did everything you threw at me, and I did it well. And you know what else? I earned the title I have now. You didn't give it to me; I *earned* it."

Her eyes flashed like a mirror in sunlight. "I never quit school, I never did drugs or had an abortion. That precious *bebé hija* of yours squandered your money, deserted the family, slept all over Dallas, fried her brain on drugs…and now you're throwing a party for her? When's my party, huh? When did you *ever* throw a party for me?"

Connie's voice shattered with anger. Tears burst from their well-guarded reservoir, angering her all the more. She wanted to be in control, to lash out; she wanted, for once, to be the favorite.

Her father shook his head. *How could she not know how much I love her?*

"Connie," he tenderly began, "you are *mi hija primera,* my firstborn daughter. Don't you know that I have always loved you? Before you were born, I loved you. And everything I own is yours. There's nothing I wouldn't give you, *mi princesa.* I've told you before, if you want for anything, all you have to do is ask.

"And as for Solana…your sister was lost to me and she found her way home. It's like she was dead all those years and has come back alive. How can I, as her father, not be happy, not throw a party to celebrate her return? I love her as I love you, Connie, Not more, not less.

He held out his hand. "Come on. Your sister is home. Let's go see her." Connie glared at him. And the band began to play.

CHAPTER 10

The Parable of the Prodigal Son

❦

At First Glance

Luke 15:11-32

Then Jesus said, "There was a man who had two sons. The younger of them said to his father, 'Father, give me the share of the property that will belong to me.' So he divided his property between them. A few days later the younger son gathered all he had and traveled to a distant country, and there he squandered his property in dissolute living. When he had spent everything, a severe famine took place throughout that country, and he began to be in need. So he went and hired himself out to one of the citizens of that country, who sent him to his fields to feed the pigs. He would gladly have filled himself with the pods that the pigs were eating; and no one gave him anything.

"But when he came to himself he said, 'How many of my father's hired hands have bread enough and to spare, but here I am dying of hunger! I will get up and go to my father, and I will say to him, "Father, I have sinned against heaven and before you; I am no longer worthy to be called your son; treat me like one of your hired hands."' So he set off and went to his father.

"But while he was still far off, his father saw him and was filled with compassion; he ran and put his arms around him and kissed him. Then the son said to him, 'Father, I have

sinned against heaven and before you; I am no longer worthy to be called your son.' But the father said to his slaves, 'Quickly, bring out a robe—the best one—and put it on him; put a ring on his finger and sandals on his feet. And get the fatted calf and kill it, and let us eat and celebrate; for this son of mine was dead and is alive again; he was lost and is found!' And they began to celebrate.

"Now his elder son was in the field; and when he came and approached the house, he heard music and dancing. He called one of the slaves and asked what was going on. He replied, 'Your brother has come, and your father has killed the fatted calf, because he has got him back safe and sound.' Then he became angry and refused to go in.

"His father came out and began to plead with him. But he answered his father, 'Listen! For all these years I have been working like a slave for you, and I have never disobeyed your command; yet you have never given me even a young goat so that I might celebrate with my friends. But when this son of yours came back, who has devoured your property with prostitutes, you killed the fatted calf for him!'

"Then the father said to him, 'Son, you are always with me, and all that is mine is yours. But we had to celebrate and rejoice, because this brother of yours was dead and has come to life; he was lost and has been found.' "

A Closer Look

This family drama, "the greatest short story ever told,"[1] is the longest and most detailed of Jesus' parables—and my favorite. As parables should, it leads to questions. How unchanged is human nature since Jesus told it? Did the Storyteller purposely avoid a predictably happy ending? Perhaps the most important question concerns its application: Where do we fit, where do I fit, in the story?

Many scholars call this the most improperly named and greatest of all New Testament parables. One scholar titles it, "The Compassionate Father and His Two Lost Sons."[2] "It would be far better if we were to call it "'The Parable of the Loving Father,'" wrote William Barclay, "for it is the father and not the son who is the hero of the story."[3] Another author terms it "the story of the Profligate Son."[4] I am inclined to call it "Papa Loves His Girls."

Nearly every sermon I've heard on this passage emphasized the younger son and the theme of repentance. But, as we know from the previous parables, each character has an equal role, and one should not receive greater emphasis than any other. In truth, these two siblings were quite similar: both were self-absorbed, both chose estrangement from those who loved them, neither respected their father or each other. The father, however, remained devoted to each child and never condemned their behavior. He loved his children "enough to allow them the freedom to make their own decisions."[5] His attitude toward them was "not determined by their character, but his."[6]

This portrait of God as a loving father was quite a departure from the expected demeanor of a distinguished Hebrew patriarch. Nor did his fictional sons behave in proper Hebrew ways. The father immediately shattered all stereotypes when he granted his child's request by settling his estate. Though unusual, a wealthy father in that era could execute his will before his death in order to retire from the business or spend his evening years in leisure. But the first-century hearers of this parable would have considered the son's request audacious and shocking—tantamount to wishing his father dead. We might assume that, like most young adults today, he was legitimately asking for his independence. However, in Middle Eastern culture "the universal conclusion was that the younger son hated his father and wanted him to die."[7]

Perhaps the young man wanted to cut loose from the restraints of generational tradition, freed of his familial and communal customs. Whatever propelled the son's geographic and psychological distancing, it was implicitly understood that the cash sum he obtained was to be invested, to earn interest, the capital untouched for future care of his elderly father and any family dependents, like unmarried sisters. To spend every cent showed disregard for the future, as if the father were already dead and his own death inevitable.

Various biblical translations declare the son's inheritance was wasted on "wild, riotous living" or "a life of debauchery." Read between those lines! Scripture does not record how he spent his money, only that he did so wastefully. It's obvious that some societal myths never change: happiness comes with the latest fashion and toys, adulation and fame equal respect, success is measured by possessions, freedom eliminates constraint, self-indulgence is a right. Every generation is seduced by temptations that end in death: death of relationships, death of dreams, death of a future. Comedian Robin Williams once speculated that "cocaine is God's way of saying you have too much money." This parable is God's way of saying we have too little regard for love, family, faith.

The prodigal's loss of "familial, ethnic, and religious identity...[were] evils worse than physical death."[8] Jesus purposely placed the son in a foreigner's pigsty because association with pork or a Gentile employer signified disavowal of faith, the ultimate disgrace. Had the carob pods reserved for the pigs been offered to the starving employee—and they weren't—he would have stuffed himself with the fodder. Did Jesus put the son at the very lowest level to show he loves and rescues "bottom of the barrel" sinners and apostates? In this setting, Jesus says there is no point too low, no lifestyle too offensive, no regret too deep, to keep a child mired in a filthy existence. Any prodigal can rise from any depth and begin the journey back home.

The runaway came to his senses and took inventory of his life. Owning only hopelessness, his options were to die or to return to his father. We do not know if his decision was based on destitution or moral remorse, if his return was scheming manipulation or honest repentance. Either way, he hoped for employment as a hired hand in his father's company. What once was given, he now expected to earn.

There is an interesting social commentary hidden in this section. The son, now living in a "foreign" land, received no food or care from his employer. Apparently, the boss's attitude was, "I don't care where the kid came from. He agreed to minimum wage, and his personal life isn't my problem." The son remembered that his father treated the ranch hands, the migrant field workers, the cleaning crew with benevolent respect. How are "foreigners" treated in our businesses, in our communities? Do we care where they came from, who they were, what they can contribute?

Large, ancient Palestinian estates operated with a three-tiered workforce: those generally called *bondmen* (slaves treated as a part of the family and given certain rights), *servants* (subordinates of the bondmen, belonging near the family), and lowest of all, *hired servants* (day laborers who often lived on the verge of complete destitution). The son planned to beg for a job in the lowest rank, the only position he thought he deserved. He carefully scripted a speech, assuming verbalized remorse was necessary to obtain forgiveness. But the father embraced his son before a single word of contrition was spoken. In the eyes of the father, the son's staggering return was confession.

Henri J. M. Nouwen, in his powerful book *The Return of the Prodigal Son,* interpreted their embrace as "not only a father who 'clasps his son in his arms,' but also a mother who caresses her child, surrounds him with the warmth of her body, and holds him against the womb from which he sprang."[9] Jesus presented a new vision of God; not a vengeful, punishing father, but a tender mother consoling and protecting a wounded child. In their emotional reunion, the "return of the prodigal son becomes the return to God's womb, the return to the very origins of being."[10]

The father's compassion for his child is the same emotion displayed in parables of the Good Samaritan and the Unforgiving Servant. Thomas Cahill wrote, "Jesus does not merely *feel* compassion, an emotion that can come and go and is dependent on outside forces; he *is* Compassion."[11]

By introducing the brother into the parable, Jesus added a frequently overlooked element of human nature—the power of silence. The initial silence of the elder son did not imply honor or innocence, but revealed greed and hypocrisy. Some scholars hold a rather harsh opinion of this brother, who should have served as a mediator during the family crisis. Rather than interceding, eliciting an apology, or working toward reconciliation, his restraint verified his lack of love for both his sibling and his father. His silence was motivated by his own gain, knowing that Hebrew custom gave the firstborn double the portion inherited by the other heirs. This elder son was well aware his birthright would provide him with two-thirds of his father's wealth in contrast to his younger brother's one-third. Silence, in this case, was a posture of selfishness. His desire for wealth and significance was as insatiable as his brother's.

Perhaps sibling rivalry kept his mouth closed. There is no indication that his younger brother sought his counsel or confidence before making his decision. The elder said nothing to prevent his younger brother's departure, which certainly insured his own elevation. He said nothing, he did nothing, a mute spectator to the fragmentation of his family.

But he certainly found his voice at the end of the parable. His contempt was clear in the scathing speech to his father. He did not begin with the customary address of respect or endearment. No formal "Father" or affectionate "Papa" or "Daddy." He severed any brotherly ties, referring to "your son," not "my brother." His insulting behavior continued when he refused to join the party, where his father and the guests would have expected him "to serve as a gracious host and at least pretend that he [was] pleased to see his long lost brother, who had made it back home."[12] But he did not live up to those expectations.

This bitter man was quite vocal in his comparisons between himself and his brother. "I've worked like a slave for you. I've never disobeyed your command. You gave him the fatted calf but never gave me a young goat so I might celebrate with my friends." He was well aware of the symbolism of shedding animal blood, the Jewish ritual that accompanies forgiveness and thankful sacrifice. A fatted calf, an expensive animal, was kept for special or religious events, whereas a goat was common, less than one-tenth the value. The jealous brother basically accused, "You spent more on him than on me!"

The father's generosity had only begun. The younger son was wrapped in his father's best robe, a garment of honor. A signet ring was placed on his finger, an heirloom that might have been expected by the elder son at the death of the father. A pair of sandals was the last gift, but not the least. They implied "the bestowal of freedom (slaves typically lacked shoes) and it is an act by which the slaves—by their act of placing the shoes on his feet—acknowledge him as their master."[13] The prodigal was not welcomed back as a slave, but as an heir. Fully reclothed and forgiven, he was restored to the status of a beloved son—which was incomprehensible to his elder brother.

It seems almost ironic that the firstborn, in a fit of rage, revealed the mind of a slave rather than a master of the estate. While the younger was satisfied to reposition himself as a slave at the lowest rung, the elder considered his position "a burdensome duty."[14] He felt not privileged, but forced, to follow in his father's footsteps. Amazing how moments of crisis uncover truths.

Jesus told this tale of brotherly estrangement to a murmuring group of Pharisees and scribes who questioned Jesus' association with publicans and sinners, considered the dregs of society. Listening to the story, the Pharisees may have recognized themselves in the self-righteous elder son. They obeyed God, the father, kept the rules of his house, served diligently in their responsibilities, but without love, appreciation or gratefulness. Like the elder son, they grumbled about the generosity showered on the unworthy. Bitterness, resentment, and duty were the elder son's characteristics, plus a jealousy that imposed detachment— all fitting descriptions of the Pharisees.

I imagine their disgust was barely concealed as, true to scriptural stereotype, the younger son received lavish attention and favor. To the listeners, what was "more galling than the acceptance of the prodigal...was the way he was received back! Where there should be sobriety, penance, remorse, sorrow, shame, sackcloth and ashes, etc., there is feasting and rejoicing. If the publicans and sinners are to enter the kingdom of God, let them do so with a penance, sorrow, and remorse appropriate to the severity of their sin!"[15]

Jesus, in this parable, rejected a preconceived image of God and painted over it a new portrait: a gracious father with boundless love and limitless pardon, who calls his children, prodigals or righteous, sinners or saintly, worthy or unworthy, to embrace one another in a celebration of family.

The father held center stage in this three-act drama while his children revolved around him. Jesus did not present a controlling father who forced his young son to stay home or to return. The father revealed "a divine attitude of forgiveness -in-advance that may seem indulgent and risky, but restore[d] a dead son to life."[16] He greeted his prodigal child with overwhelming compassion, just as he approached his elder son with gentle assurance of his devotion and love. This active father refused "to limit the measure of his grace to human ways of seeing and doing things."[17]

The original hearers of Jesus' story were appalled by the father's actions. First, he actually divided his estate at the bequest of an insolent child, and then, he welcomed his shameful son home with forgiveness. What stunned them mostly was not his mercy but the fact that he *ran* toward his errant son. Respectable men in the ancient world certainly did not run. Aristotle wrote, "great men never run in public."[18] In ancient culture, "the idea of the *paterfamilias* running for any reason would occasion ludicrous shock."[19] But this fictional father ran flat out, in full extent of his powers. It required hoisting his long robe, revealing hairy legs and ankles; it meant throwing dignity to the wind as he took off down the road. But this father didn't care what others thought. He only cared that his son know the love of his father.

The listeners were again shocked by the father's behavior toward the elder son. No respectable host would leave a celebration to cajole an angry child boycotting a social event. For a second time, the compassion of the father superseded expectation, for by law, he had the right to put his rebellious son to death, just as he could have stoned the stubborn prodigal for his behavior. Instead, his love eclipsed the rigidity of law. Throughout the whole story, the issue of legality was present. But the father dismissed judicial punishment in favor of unifying forgiveness. He was more concerned with his children than his honor. He was intent on family reconciliation and would do anything to bring it about.

This parabolic father broke all the molds. What kind of parent says "it's necessary" to have a party? The necessity of a full-blown celebration was doubly stated, ensuring everyone understood the magnitude of this father's joy: "This son of mine was dead and is alive again." Twice the father uttered this dramatic phrase. But there is only one Son of whom it can truly be said, *He was dead and is alive.*[20] The Son of God descended to the same depths as the fictitious son, to rescue and redeem all prodigals. This Son suffered the child's degradation and shame in order to reconcile him with his family. "It is compassion for the lost that brings about life out of death and that makes restoration—even transformation—possible in people's lives."[21]

The father's final words to his elder son, "you are always with me and all that is mine is yours," showed affectionate companionship, co-ownership, and an unbreakable bond, a fitting conclusion to the story. This exemplary father may not have approved of the actions, choices, or attitudes of his children, but he was forever and inextricably present in their lives. This father loved beyond comprehension. He cared not one whit about public opinion; he cared for the physical, emotional, and psychological welfare of his children. His sons and daughters were always welcome in his magnanimous heart. The doors of his house were an open invitation to eat and to dance, to celebrate and to laugh together in a bond of family unity. This loving parent was Jesus' portrait of his heavenly Father. And ours.

CHAPTER 11

Looking Beyond Freedom

Behind the Image

This is a story fit for twenty-first-century runaways and exiles. Ancient and modern families have been torn apart by the issues prominent in the parable. Why do girls and boys run away from home? Often for good reason. My husband and I attended a wedding reception where we introduced ourselves to the bride's father and complimented him on his daughter's talent and beauty, her well-deserved, high-profile job. He nodded in impatient agreement, then interrupted to say, "Yes, yes, but my other girl, now *she's* the beautiful and talented one." For several minutes, he bragged about his "other" daughter. No wonder the bride was estranged from her parents and had invited them to the wedding only out of a sense of duty.

Solana—The Younger Daughter

The story of Solana illustrates our tendency to seek attention or simply independence away from home. We flee restrictions and confinement of family where we feel pigeon-holed in inescapable boxes. We believe that money will solve our problems and are deluded by the myth that expensive possessions represent worth. We are certain that luxuries will bring us happiness, or at least reduce stress. We regularly play the "if only" game: If only I had more cash, if only I lived someplace else, if only I had a better job, *then* I would be secure, happy, fulfilled. Solana learned that money buys an illusion of success. Even with a fortune at her disposal, she could not obtain her intangible goals. She was the personification of Luke 12:34, "Where your treasure is, there your heart will be also." Sophistication and admiration were the glittering treasures of her heart, and the price she paid pursuing them was destruction.

Solana in Dallas reminds me of Eve in the garden. Both women had expectations of what they would be like after making intentional choices. They anticipated a better, freer, less constrained life. They thought they would become different, more powerful, more in control. Both women fell for the enemy's ultimate lie and the results proved tragic. What they expected and what they actually received were two different things, culminating in their ruin.

A popular fashion magazine recently reported on the life of a British heiress. After receiving her inheritance, she immediately moved to London and into an unrestrained lifestyle. By age twenty-seven every pound and every shilling was squandered. How many years passed before every dollar, every cent of Solana's inheritance was spent?

Solana fought the truth until she could no longer avoid reality. Only at her personal bottom, broke and starving, did she say, "I will get up and go to my father." *I will get up.* At the point of complete despair, she could remain down and die—or get up and live. How hard is it to say *I will get up?* How hard is it to admit that wallowing in a bad situation or relationship is easier than risking change; that working in a dead-end job is easier than going back to school; that hanging with a familiar but harmful crowd is easier than finding a new group of friends. Solana had a powerful reason to get up. A father, a home, were waiting for her.

I will go to my father. Originally, she exchanged her place in the family for money. She abandoned her loving parent for the lure of excitement. Only desperation and hunger changed her perspective. She hoped to re-establish herself as her father's child, but not as a *loved* child; the best she could hope for was a position in his company as a day laborer, an hourly worker.

All the way home, Solana planned the details of their reunion; where she would stand, where he would stand, what she would say, what he would say. We often imagine confrontations as a way of controlling the circumstances. We sift through options, script the best lines, polish and hone the dialogue to manipulate the outcome. We carefully choose our words, anticipating our opponent's stammering reactions. In my imaginary conversations, I'm always eloquent and witty, the verbal victor. Most of these exchanges never actually happen, but the mental dramatization fortifies my sense of power, my need to be right, my necessity to win the vocal showdown.

Why was Solana so intent to compose a perfect script? She feared what many children fear: a parent's "I told you so." To avoid that indictment, she immediately launched into her speech. "Daddy, I'm sorry. I sinned against heaven and in your sight. I am no longer worthy to be called your daughter." Her anticipation of his anger, judgment, and vindictiveness justified her rehearsed speech. But her father couldn't stand to hear his beloved daughter utter those demeaning words and he immediately cut short her confession.

Solana pictured her future as an insignificant employee, but her father welcomed her as a daughter. His benevolence far exceeded her expectation. She was welcomed with open arms, without judgment. There was no "I told you so," no withering look of disgust, no banishment to employee housing. Why did she assume the worst? Why do we "prodigal children" doubt the possibility of restoration?

Safe in the house of her father, Solana found love and acceptance. But was she fully accepted and valued at home? Not by her sister, Connie.

Constancia—The Elder Daughter

Who wants to admit being like Connie? Firstborn children often arrive to a welcome of high standards and spend their entire lives trying to "live up to the expectations of their parents and be considered obedient and dutiful. They want to please. They often fear disappointing their parents. Some also experience, quite early in life, a certain envy toward their younger brothers and sisters, who seem to be less concerned about pleasing and much freer in 'doing their own thing.' "[1]

It appears that initially Connie worked hard to validate her birthright. Somewhere along the line, she viewed the generous inheritance from her father as payment for her diligence. A bequest became a burden. What was Connie's motivation to dependably carry on the family business? Prestige? Duty? In this character, we see that "one cannot serve God merely for the sake of personal benefit or for the sake of receiving a reward and of avoiding punishment."[2] Our service to God comes from a position of privilege and humbleness, not obligation or duty.

Connie's stable, perfectly structured life collapsed at the return of her sister. How often do smooth lives get snarled by the embarrassing behaviors of an irritating family member? When a sibling's life careens off course, it can plunge the entire family into a nightmare. It's hoped that compassion would surface in such situations, that love would sacrifice for the benefit of the wounded, but that is not often the case. Connie's first-child concern proved personal: How will this affect me, my schedule, my reputation, my future?

Maybe Connie's real fear was that her sister would get more than her fair share. The property was already divided, two-thirds of it placed in Connie's name. Solana chose to squander her inheritance. Did Connie assume that her father would ask her to share her portion with Solana? Good grief, would she have to employ her sister? What a horrifying possibility: hiring an unreliable, irresponsible sibling, sharing not only a surname but perhaps even an office.

Connie asked a delivery truck driver what was going on
in her own house. Why did she ask a stranger about the
reason for the party? Why didn't she go directly to her father
with her questions? Why do we turn to people outside the
family, allowing their opinions to inform and influence our
responses? Too often, we base our conclusions on their limited or cynical observations, measure our lives by their
morals, their philosophies, their ethics. We accept information
from a segment of society that doesn't know or appreciate
the dynamics of our heritage, our faith, our family. Why do
we older sisters avoid going to the Father for truth?

It's obvious that rumors of Solana's behavior in Dallas had
reached Connie. Otherwise, where did she get her accusatory
information? How did she know her sister had squandered
her money, slept all over Dallas, overdosed on drugs? It
appears Connie pulled out her treasure chest of accusations
and purposefully reaffixed the old labels, branding Solana
with a "bad girl" reputation. Even if Connie's assessment was
correct, will she give her sister another chance? Did she view
her sibling's homecoming as a fresh start or a sham?

What amazes me about this part of the story is Connie's
lack of curiosity. Wasn't she just a wee bit curious to see
Solana? How much weight she had gained or lost? How
wrinkled or worn she looked? Connie's detachment indicated
total severance of their relationship. But not for long. Dormant
feelings of animosity rose the moment her father confronted
her with his good news.

Connie instantly launched into her "I" section. "I never, I
didn't, I wasn't..." Isn't comparison a common human
behavior? Informed of others' failings, we bristle with indignation and retort, "I certainly wouldn't have..." Connie was
so sure of her superiority, her right to anger and disgust, that
she refused to enter her own home since her father's
daughter was inside. The consequence of her hatred was
self-imposed exile.

The telling moment came when Connie asked her father, "When did you ever throw a party for me?" Jealousy, bitterness, resentment dripped off every word. By her question, one who was so externally rich showed great poverty of the soul. Like Connie, do we yell at God, "You did that for *her,* why won't you do that for *me?*"

The father tried to erase Connie's sense of inequality. The reason for the party, he said, is because "your sister" is home. It was that simple and that wonderful. Today, we host parties when someone graduates, gets promoted, earns special recognition for an accomplishment. God rejoices in the company and in the return of his children.

I struggle to understand why Connie stood outside her father's love. What convinced her that her place in the family, her self-worth, was measured by her work, her being the "good girl?" Was it her lack of understanding of her father's love that made her insecure? If Jesus' parables represent daily life, how common is this behavior of "earning" our place, even our salvation? What good works do we hold up, attempting to justify or earn our place in the Father's family?

The Father—The Doting Papa

This portrait of the forgiving father "captures the gospel in miniature."[3] In the biblical story, the father gave shape to the parable. "At each point, from the granting of the initial son's request to the 'going out' to the elder brother, the father's actions allow the narrative to unfold and provide its crucial turning points. Who the father is, however, and how he acts, are also dependent on how the sons act, and the drama arises from observing not only what the father does but what the sons will do."[4]

The lost daughter found her way back home largely because of what her father *didn't* say. He did not say, "If you leave this house, don't expect to come back. If you walk out that door, it's for good." Nor did he mock her adventurous spirit. The years of parental control and instruction had come to an end, and he allowed his daughter to leave his protection, to stand or fall as an adult making her own choices. He granted her freedom, though he obviously knew what was in store. He also knew the futility of additional warnings. Was his "letting go" an act of love? Is being freed to fail a grace?

Years later, when Solana imagined her return to the father, she anticipated harsh restitution. In her mind, the father "might have said, 'That's all very well, young [lady]; we have heard fine speeches before. Now you buckle to and get down to work as you have never worked before, and if we see that you really mean what you say, we may let you work your passage. But you can never make good the damage you have done to the family's good name and property.' That in itself would have been an act of grace; it might have done the young [wo]man a world of good and [her] elder [sister] would probably not have objected. But—and this is the point of the parable—that is not how God treats sinners. He does not put them on probation first, to see how they will turn out. He welcomes them with overflowing love and generosity."[5]

The loving father didn't live by our rules or act according to the expectations of his children. He was not vengeful or antagonistic; he was a weeping, running, hugging embodiment of love. He recognized his daughter even though she had aged and lost her beauty. He kissed his smelly and dirty baby girl and held her close. He laughed with sheer joy at her return. He didn't care what shape she was in; he cared that she was home. Author Brennan Manning often says that "the Father loves us as we are and not as we should be, since none of us is as we should be."[6]

The father showed equal compassion for his firstborn, a different kind of prodigal. The original hearers of this parable expected "the father to reject the elder son for his protest at the younger son's reception. [When he] instead responds, 'Child, you are always with me and all that is mine is yours'— [it is] a profound shock to the audience's expectations."[7] While the younger fled to a foreign country, the elder remained home, emotionally, relationally, and physically on the outside. Both children were allowed the freedom to make decisions and to experience the consequences. The father did not prefer one child over the other; both were chosen, both were loved, and he obviously longed for their unity. In every scene, he is shown as "the Father of compassion and the God of all comfort who comforts us in all our troubles."[8] Compassion literally means to "come alongside." Our heavenly Father stands beside us in our misery, our contempt, our failure, even in our arrogance, haughtiness, and indifference. He is not as concerned with what we have been as much as what we will become.

The father cherished his children even in their aversion to one another. The sisters disregarded one another in their separate, independent lives. Solana departed without a word to her sister; Connie referred to her sibling as her father's daughter. These two women viewed one another as competitors rather than companions. So many of us tend to treat other women suspiciously, guardedly. We believe we must first and foremost promote ourselves. "Our culture says that ruthless competition is the key to success. Jesus says that ruthless compassion is the purpose of our journey."[9] Women, whether related by blood or spirit, are called to sisterhood in the house of their father.

But this father seems too good to be true. Many fathers these days have too much to do, have too many things to think about and are much too tired to drive to the grocery store, let alone slaughter the fatted calf. Many adult daughters long for a father like Solana and Connie's: a father who refuses to judge or condemn obvious and self-apparent mistakes, a father who does not punish us when we are so apt, so willing, to punish ourselves and to justify our punishment of others. We wish for a father who treats his daughters equally. We ache for a father who celebrates us.

Jesus says that the Father is waiting. Waiting for us with open arms. With unconditional and limitless love. He is waiting for us to enter his house, to humbly embrace our brothers and sisters, to eat the feast of forgiveness, and to dance to the music of grace. The Father waits for us to join the eternal celebration of coming home.

Seeing Ourselves

As an admitted prodigal in my younger years, I see my own reflection in Solana's attitudes and behaviors. Like her, I wanted independent freedom from my family, and, like her, I abandoned my faith for a wild, unrestricted life. Only when the consequence of my choices left me wallowing in self-destruction did I realize that my only hope was to return to God and ask for forgiveness. I will never forget the day of my "homecoming" and the joy of friends who prayed with me. From that day to this, my life is drastically different. I can't say that it's always been "happily ever after," but certainly I am at peace and contented in the company of an extended spiritual family.

We're not sure of what happened next in Solana's life, since this parable doesn't have a "wrap-up" ending. Did Connie go into the house to greet Solana? We do not know. Was the father able to successfully mediate peace between his daughters? Did the sisters grow to love each other? Your guess is as good as mine. On all counts, I hope so.

In our own story, do we treat God like a Supreme Trust Fund? Is our love for him conditioned by what he gives to us? Do we really think that we can love the Father but not love our imperfect brothers and sisters? In this story, God places greater importance on love and family unity than on absolute obedience.

Since parables are told so we might see ourselves, who are you in the story? Are you the younger daughter, waking up to the fact that you're no longer sleeping on satin sheets?

Is your dream lost in a haze of excess and self-centeredness? Have you lost or depleted everything you once valued? Are you ready to get up and go home?

Do you see yourself in the resentful elder sister, standing outside, yelling, "What about me?" Are you willing to leave bitterness outside and step into the house of the father's love? Have you ever stood outside church doors, office buildings, school yards, or someone else's home, self-exiled because he, she, or they were inside? Refused to attend a family reunion or a party because a divorced relative was there with a new partner? Our critical commentary is not limited to family. Pride or haughtiness makes us say things like, "I can't believe she has the nerve to wear a white wedding dress!" "Why did she get the solo?" "The promotion should have gone to me, not her!" Are you guilty of buddying up to strangers in order to gather information about others, whom you then openly criticize and denounce?

Or, do your actions and attitudes mirror those of the father? In this parable, God is a mature parent who watches out the window, who stands in the middle of the road; a parent who looks and waits for prodigals who return with diseases, addictions, failures, and crippling fears. Are you the one who stands in the middle of the street, arms stretched wide, a haven of grace and forgiveness? Does your voice echo through the dark night of despair, calling, "Come here, come into my arms. Here you will find love, here you will find compassion, here you will find mercy"? Do you whisper the comforting words, "Welcome home, my beloved brother, my beloved sister"?

Are you able to believe that the return of a prodigal is actually reason enough for immediate celebration? The father did. Who do you know that needs an invitation to a party celebrating a fresh start? Who needs to see such joy from you on their behalf?

In truth, we have been the younger. In our foolishness, we abandon the truth to chase an attractive lie. We leave our

Father's side, our family, to follow an illusion. Our lives crumble in despair and loss, estranged from those who love us. Often we act like the elder. In our esteemed position as "firstborn," we mock the naiveté of the young. We hold up our success, our wealth, our importance as personal flags of greatness. We snub outsiders who are less educated, less affluent, less apt to acknowledge our prominence.

Whether younger or elder, we are challenged to make the intentional decision to follow the progression of maturity. We are to become the parent. We leave our childishness behind. We put away our quest for self-importance. We open our arms with compassion and run without concern of public opinion. We go out to meet both prodigals and perfectionists without judgment and welcome them inside the house of unconditional love. We aim to become like the father, the very image of God.

CHAPTER 12

Reflections of Acceptance

❦

How easy is it to identify with either a younger or elder sister? Sometimes, not even a look in the mirror will reveal our true identity. I have to confess that I did not recognize myself for the first two months I worked on this chapter.

I spoke on the prodigal parable at a women's retreat in Virginia Beach. In conclusion, I reminded the audience that we must choose the character that best represents us. Then I asked, "So which woman are you? Are you the younger sister? Are you the elder?" As soon as the word "elder" left my lips, an accusatory *Yes!* screamed in my mind. I paused; the audience thought for dramatic effect. In truth, I was trying not to collapse from the shock of truth.

For many years, I was a business associate and friend to a man with a history of failed marriages and relationships. When he announced his engagement to a much younger woman, I was quick to disapprove for both professional and personal reasons. I knew that this marriage could have repercussions in our field of Christian ministry and directly affect my work. I was all too familiar with his track record and feared inevitable marital failure. Emotionally, I didn't want to go through it with him again.

For the sake of his reputation, his future, and his spiritual life, I begged him to reconsider, as did others who loved him. Disregarding advice and showing no concern for the ramifications, he married after a short courtship.

Six months after their wedding, I attended a conference, along with the newlyweds and about seventy-five others. It was the first official introduction and appearance of the bride into this pre-established group. Some attendees greeted the "new wife" warmly; others were coolly distant. She tried her best to endear herself to everyone, especially to me.

On the second day, I hosted a special luncheon for about twenty women. The conversation was pleasant, and I purposely directed questions to make sure everyone had an opportunity to speak. All but one. Halfway through the meal, I noticed the new wife abruptly sit back in her chair; there she quietly stayed for the rest of the meal. When it was over, she charged toward me like a bullet. "Can we talk?" she asked. I cringed. Everything within me wanted to say, "No," but several of the other women overheard her request, so I sweetly demurred. "Sure," I smiled, thinking it would never happen.

But it did happen. We sat down at an outdoor table in the early afternoon. Her first question nearly knocked me over. With an unfaltering gaze, she said, "I know you love everyone here. Why can't you love me?"

Ingoring her question, I gave the answer I wanted her to hear. Without a trace of graciousness, I took it upon myself to tell her why I opposed this marriage, why I was so angry at her husband. I told her that she had refused to see the truth, that she had willingly been deceived. I suggested that she allowed her husband's prestige to fog her logic.

She interrupted now and then to ask specific, clarifying questions. I bluntly answered them as she tried to retain her dignity.

But that one question hung in the air: "Why can't you love me?" Nearly three hours after we began, I was emotionally exhausted. It had all been said. After a minute or two of silence, she dared to voice it again. "Why can't you love *me?*" The other stuff didn't matter to her. She had made her choice. From her perspective, right or wrong, she was now a member of this extended business family. She was looking into the future and wanted to know her place in it, especially in relationship to me.

"I can't love you." The answer flew out of me. "I *do* like you, and I know that we could become friends. But in a few years, I'm afraid you will be discarded and divorced, and I will be left in the mess. You will be gone." I barely choked out the last few words, "I will miss you, and my heart will break. I don't know if I can do it again."

There it was: the truth. It surprised me as much as it did her.

I wish I could confess that we embraced and became close friends. Only half would be true. We did embrace. But we did not become friends. I was polite and mannerly when forced to meet in business situations. But I did not love her.

My husband and I eventually moved to another state. I left the past and happily ensconced myself in writing, speaking, and producing albums—on sisterhood. The irony escaped me.

Through the grapevine, I heard that the couple had a child. But rarely did I think of them, and when I heard their names in conversation, I usually thought some acerbic comment.

One day a phone call relayed news of their impending divorce. I hung up, walked to my bedroom, fell on the bed and began to cry. My emotions ping-ponged from extreme sadness for her, to anger at her husband, to remorse for my own actions. I deeply regretted that I had been cruel in our conversation, that my prediction proved true, that I had refused the opportunity to love a woman brought into my life for a season.

Now I had specific, burning questions: Who helped her through those years of marital despair? Who counseled her? What series of events ended a marriage and separated an infant from its father? I cried for the loss of a marriage, the breakup of yet another family, the thought of what might have been. But I *did* nothing. I did not write or call her. The initial shock wore off and life went on. At times I thought of her and wondered how she was managing. Still I did nothing.

Then, several years later, I stood at that podium in Virginia Beach, teaching women from the parable of prodigal sisters. "Are you the younger," I asked. "Are you the elder?" I nearly buckled under the weight of guilt. I was like David, when Nathan quietly said, "You are the man." I admitted, right then, "I am the elder." In the unflinching mirror of truth, I saw that I am judgmental and haughty, cruel and compassionless. I am self-righteous and self-serving. I am the elder sister, and I am sorry.

The original parable does not have a happy, tidy ending. Did the elder sister go in and embrace the younger? We do not know. The choice was left to her and her alone. Just as the choice is left to me, to us. We write the ending to our own stories. I vowed in front of the audience that I would try to find my younger sister, that I would send a letter or phone or e-mail to ask for forgiveness, that I would admit my sin, my hypocrisy, my arrogance. It may be too late to offer my love now. She may abhor my attempt and reject me as I rejected her. The damage may be irreparable. But I am trying to write a new ending to my story. I am committed to living the lesson learned from the parable: our lives are a process of maturity, involving the younger, the elder, the loving parent. I have been the younger, I have been the elder, but I want my story to end with a new portrait. I aim to become like the Father, the very image of God.

Study Guide

Study Guide

❧

The Image of Compassion

1. We have just entered the third millennium since Jesus told his parable of a neighbor. "[If] we had followed in the humble footsteps of a heretical Samaritan who was willing to wash someone else's wounds, rather than in the self-regarding steps of the priest and the immaculate steps of the Levite—the world we inhabit would be a very different one."[1]

   Do you agree with the above statement? Do you find it difficult to separate theological and practical concerns for others? How might the two be resolved? Can you cite other scriptural instances of being called to the work of kindness? Why is it so important? How would the world, your city, your community, your family, be different if you were more like the Samaritan?

2. In Jesus' day, Jews frequently debated the meaning of "neighbor," generally agreeing it included fellow Jews and full proselytes. But the strict Pharisees tended to exclude non-Pharisees; the elitist Essenes required everyone inside their narrowly confined sect to "hate all the sons of darkness"[2]—meaning nearly everyone but themselves. God's chosen people, at least the doctrinally diligent ones, had become a harsh, critical group, certain that God's favor rested on a select devout few and remained absent from sinners and/or Gentiles.

   Who do you consider a neighbor? Who is not your neighbor? What is the difference?

3. Different sects within Judaism couldn't agree on the definition of "neighbor." They not only excluded "outsiders" or non-Jews, but excluded each other.

   Are we elitist today? Do we avoid those of different faiths or denominations? Do we determine who is "saved" and who deserves eternal damnation? From reading this parable, what does God expect from our treatment of one another? Has your own behavior, your choice of responses to others, changed as a result of this story?

4. Jews despised the Samaritans, who observed the Torah but not the Prophets, "who worshiped not in the Jerusalem Temple but in [their own temple on] Mount Gerizim. There is no hatred so intense as *odium theologicum*—hatred for those nearby who are religiously similar to oneself but nonetheless different."[3]

   Do you respect people whose religious beliefs oppose Christian tenets? Can you recall any example of Jesus' reaction to those outside the Jewish faith? How did he treat them? What can you learn from that? Discuss denominational isolation or sectarianism within the realm of Christianity and how important or divisive they have become.

5. "Our spiritual life cannot be measured by success as the world measures it, but only by what God pours through us—and we cannot measure that at all."[4] Rachel's testimony about her physical addiction and spiritual redemption became her ministry which became a business. Her "success" caused estrangement from her family and church. She considered speaking, writing, and teaching,

her "calling," her main responsibilities—and anything outside those parameters was delegated to others.

Could Rachel have avoided her dilemma? How do you respond to her predicament? Have you thought about the struggles and demands placed upon your own spiritual leaders? What is required for any of us to rightly prioritize all the aspects of personal and spiritual development: marriage, parenthood, education, career, Christian maturity, and service? How do you measure success? How are you like Rachel?

6. Faith excelled in every area of her life. She was competent and proficient, yet she positioned herself in Rachel's shadow. Each day was managed with lists, a detailed schedule, preplanned goals. Efficiency was honed to perfection. But when something happened out of her control, fear and disdain kept her from touching Anya.

Do you find yourself attempting only things in which you will succeed? Do you consider other vocations or talents more glamorous, superior, to your own? How does pride motivate or underlie your choices? In what areas do you try to control people and life? Have you ever withheld empathy because the "victims" deserved their fate? Are you motivated by what others think, how they will judge you? How are you like Faith?

7. Sammi broke the stereotypical, preconceived notions that described a Samaritan. She set aside her own goals to raise her nephew; set aside her schedule to care for a stranger. She paid cash for Anya's care and tenderly washed her battered body. She corresponds to Jesus' model of compassion.

Are you tempted to dismiss non-Christians as "them" as opposed to "us"? Do you assume groups labeled by race, ethnicity, social class, religion, or lack of religion, are predictably alike? What would it take for you to spontaneously set aside your own schedule for someone else's sake? How do you react when a non-believer acts "Christian"? What kind of person would you have chosen for the Samaritan character? Are any people in our culture as hated as the Samaritans? Why do you think Jesus chose a Samaritan?

8. "It is not enough simply to enter the world of the neighbor with care and compassion; one must enter and leave it in such a way that the neighbor is given freedom along with the very help that is offered."[5] Under Sammi's care, Anya was granted not only physical care but also freedom from slavery and debt.

    How can we "free" people at risk? Is the annual donation to the homeless mission the same thing? Does writing a monthly check to an aid organization free the poor or appease your conscience? How do you justify your lack of personal involvement? What are your reasons for not getting your hands dirty?

9. Anya represents Christ in the parable with her wounds, abandonment, pain, and suffering.

    How easy or difficult is it to recognize Christ in the guise of others? When or how do you speak for the voiceless, provide power for the powerless, financially sustain the poor? When you find yourself wounded, abandoned, and suffering in pain, do you consider yourself Christ-like? Would you allow someone to carry you to safety, to healing, to freedom? Or are you inclined to pull yourself out of the ditch? Why?

10. Parables require that we find ourselves in the story. Each character had both strong and weak traits, correct and flawed thinking, admirable or reproachable behavior, and justifiable reasons for her choices.

   In this parable of a "Good" Samaritan, who do you resemble? What is required for you to live like the Samaritan in your community?

The Image of Forgiveness

1. When Jacob and Esau meet for the first time after a lengthy estrangement, Jacob says to his brother, " 'I have seen your face as one sees the face of God' " (Gen. 33:10 Fox). "If we have ever truly been forgiven," wrote Kathleen Norris, "if we've ever been on the receiving end of an act of mercy that made a difference in our lives, we have seen the face of God."[6]

   Recall an instance when were you on the receiving end of mercy. What difference did it make in your life? When have you been on the giving end of mercy? What difference did it make both in your life and in the recipient's life?

2. In Matthew 16:23, Jesus accused Peter of setting his mind "not on divine things but on human things."

   What are divine things? What are human things? How do they differ? What is your mind set on? How do we discipline our minds to give appropriate attention to divine things when human things are so immediate?

3. Jesus instructed his followers, in Matthew 5:23-26, to reconcile with "your brother or sister" before offering gifts to God and to "come to terms" with an accuser before going to court.

   Is this directive still applicable today? Do you know anyone who has something against you? Have you tried to settle the dispute? Does "coming to terms" apply only to financial disputes? Explain the importance of "leave your gift there before the altar and go; first be reconciled."

4. Justine reflected the image of God by lavishly forgiving a woman's entire debt. She forgave for two reasons: she had the authority and she was asked.

   Has anyone asked you for forgiveness? How did you respond? Why? What resources are at your disposal that you might generously give to others, whether or not asked? How are you like Justine?

5. Elena's refusal to forgive was not a spur-of-the-moment decision; it was the result of a lifetime of self-centeredness, self-indulgence, and self-importance. Her "right" to collect debt verified the Proverbs 14:12 observation: "There is a way that seems right to a person, but its end is the way to death."

   Have you ever refused to forgive someone? What were the consequences to you, to him/her? What keeps you from forgiving them now? Are there still material things or personal relationships that you refuse to share, convinced of your "right" to withhold? How are you like Elena?

6. Karyn was exhausted by her efforts to keep her family intact. One disaster followed another, yet she diligently worked to provide for her daughters and herself.

   Have you ever had a season when one crisis followed another? How did you respond emotionally, physically, spiritually? How did others either help or hinder your situation? Do you know anyone like Karyn? How could you help her? How are you like Karyn?

7. Gabriella, Justine's assistant, admired and emulated her employer. In the event of injustice, she ran to Justine, expecting the older woman to restore justice.

   Is there a younger woman in your life who watches your every move, who desires to be like you? Do you consider her attention a nuisance or a responsibility? Are you a model of justice and mercy? Is there an older woman in your life who is more like Elena than Justine, a model of "what not to do"? How are you like Gabriella?

8. Read Romans 13:8-10. "Let no debt remain outstanding, except the continuing debt to love one another." Read John 15:12. "Love one another as I have loved you."

   Describe your idea of a "debt of love." To whom is it due and how is it paid? How has Christ loved you? Is it possible to love others as he loves?

9. In the original parable, the verdict for the unforgiving servant was a harsh enactment of James 2:13: "For judgment will be without mercy to anyone who has shown no mercy."

Does this image of God's swift judgment contradict images of a compassionate, merciful God? How do you explain that Jesus told us to forgive repeatedly, then promptly condemned the unforgiving servant after only one failure?

10. Justine and Elena have independence and abundant wealth in common, but they couldn't be more different. Gabrie and Karyn each play dependent but responsible roles in this story.

    Which character, in this parable of divine forgiveness, best represents you? Why? Whether or not you are in a formal position of power, what do you need to do to resemble Justine?

11. C.S. Lewis wrote, "To forgive the incessant provocations of daily life—to keep on forgiving the bossy mother-in-law, the bullying husband, the nagging wife, the selfish daughter, the deceitful son—how can we do it? Only, I think, by remembering where we stand, by meaning our words when we say in our prayers each night, 'Forgive us our trespasses as we forgive those that trespass against us.' We are offered forgiveness on no other terms. To refuse it is to refuse God's mercy for ourselves."[7]

    When you recite the Lord's Prayer, do you sincerely believe that God will forgive you in the same way you forgive others? Is "debt" synonymous only with "sin," or does it also refer to money? What if God answered your prayer and forgave you as you forgave others?

The Image of Humility

1. In Romans 12:3, Paul wrote: "For by the grace given to me I say to everyone among you not to think of yourself more highly than you ought to think, but to think with sober judgment, each according to the measure of faith that God has assigned."

   Isn't it natural, even healthy, to think well of oneself? What does Paul mean? Does the reference to the Body of Christ in Romans 12:4-13 correlate with equality? Why or why not?

2. "I believe that the first test of a truly great man is his humility. I do not mean by humility, doubt of his own powers. But really great men have a curious feeling that the greatness is not in them, but through them. And they see something divine in every other man and are endlessly, foolishly, incredibly merciful."[8]

   How do you determine greatness in others? Do you believe "something divine" exists in every person? Why does the author combine humility with mercy?

3. On more than one occasion, the disciples vied for position. "An argument arose among them as to which one of them was the greatest. But Jesus, aware of their inner thoughts, took a little child and put it by his side, and said to them, 'Whoever welcomes this child in my name welcomes me, and whoever welcomes me welcomes the one who sent me; for the least among all of you is the greatest.' " (Luke 9:46-48).

Why is position, the desire to be great, so important? How is humility equated to little children, and what is their example to adults clamoring for recognition?

4. "In respect of civil rights, all citizens are equal before the law. The humblest is the peer of the most powerful."[9]

   Equality for citizens is explicit in the U.S. Constitution, but is it practiced in reality? Can you think of an example when a poor citizen had equal power to a rich citizen? Why does inequality still exist if we believe the principle to be true?

5. Susan was forced to resign her position due to her husband's transfer, a common occupational hazard.

   How well do you accept change, especially when caused by a child or spouse? How easily do you adapt to changing seasons of life? How do you feel when things go well without you?

6. Darlene's inability to see herself as others saw her caused problems for Lily and Charlotte. What she saw in herself and what others saw were diametrically opposed.

   Do you think you have an honest perspective of your abilities, personality, character traits? When you're harshly accused of things like being controlling, uptight, careless, or irresponsible, do you consider the possibility of that being true?

7. Charlotte is the example of humility being exalted.

   Have you ever been unexpectedly honored? Or humbled?
   Were you deserving of such treatment? How would
   you describe the fine line between humility and self-
   deprecation? How do you feel when others are lauded
   and you are ignored? How do you treat others after
   you are honored?

8. The fictional women in Braden County sponsored a conference to unite Christian women of their community.

   Has your town, neighborhood, or community attempted
   an all-inclusive event? Did a wide variety of churches or
   organizations participate or was the event polarized by
   labels of denomination or race? Did you try again?

9. Racial and societal inequality still exist in public schools,
   communities, businesses, and unfortunately, even in
   churches.

   What possibilities do you see for reaching across barriers of economics, religion, education, regional prejudices? How do you humble yourself and exalt those
   considered "more lowly"? How do you respond when
   such a gesture is rebuffed? Does that deter your efforts?

10. Lavish banquets are usually costly and require an enor-
    mous amount of planning.

    Does Jesus literally or figuratively mean for you to feed
    the poor? At what cost? In what ways can you invite the
    "uninvitable" crippled, blind, and lame to a feast?

11. When this parable was told, Jesus certainly knew who he was, yet the other guests assumed he belonged at a lower place.

    Do you think Jesus' feelings were hurt? Was he angry when he told the parable, or mildly amused and intent on setting the social record straight? How do you react when socially snubbed or not given due respect? Do you extend to others the same courteous respect that you desire?

12. Chuck Colson wrote that "the Christian life cannot be lived alone. To follow Christ is to become part of a new community."[10]

    What are the traits of an inclusive community? Exclusive community? How do we keep a flexible community from becoming rigid?

The Image of Grace

1. The story of the prodigal in Luke closely parallels Joseph's story in Genesis. Both sons lived in a foreign land subsequently plagued by famine; both rushed to meet their approaching father and fell on his neck; both were given a ring and fine linen garments.

   Is the prodigal parable a New Testament retelling of Joseph's life? Why or why not? What would prompt Jesus' modernization of the story?

2. Pharaoh confessed to Moses, "I have sinned against the LORD your God and against you" (Exodus 10:16). Hosea's

wife said, "I will go and return to my first husband, for it was better for me than now" (Hosea 2:7).

What does Jesus accomplish by including these references in the parable?

3. Against tradition, "younger sons are chosen by God for important roles in sacred history....[They] live apart from the expected lines of power and authority, and in choosing them God reverses normal human expectations. Such people are symbols of those who receive the unexpected and unmerited favor of God."[11]

Does Jesus challenge the Hebrew tradition of favoring the firstborn son? What is the reason for your answer?

4. The influence of this parable on fiction is traced back to the sixteenth century.[12] Shakespeare alludes to this parable more than to any other.[13] Esteemed authors make reference[14] as do notable poets.[15] "It has been a subject for great painters (Dürer), dramatists (Gascoigne), choreographers (Balanchine), musicians (Prokofiev, Britten), and philosophers (Nietzsche).

What is the universal appeal of this story? Why do stories work better than straight facts to influence us?

5. William Faulkner wrote that man "is immortal, not because he alone among creatures has an inexhaustible voice, but because he has a soul, a spirit capable of compassion and sacrifice and endurance." Compassion literally means to "come alongside."

What is the conditional requirement of 2 Corinthians 1:3-4? How do you evaluate your own capability to offer compassion? Is it easy or difficult for you to give yourself to another? How do you "come alongside" prodigals and their siblings?

6. Even though it seems extreme, Solana represents many children who want independence and autonomy from the family.

   If you have ever unwisely demanded your own way, was it ultimately beneficial for you? What were the consequences? How hard is it to admit that your expectations turned into disappointments? How are you like Solana? Do you know a Solana?

7. Lucinda and Rush manipulated, duped, and swindled Solana. Their greed stole more than cash or furniture; they robbed Solana of her trust. They took advantage of her naiveté and her hunger for attention.

   Have you ever been deceived by such "friends"? Is it possible to warn others against these types of people? Did Solana deserve the treatment she received? Why or why not? Have you envied another person's wealth, talent, skills, or opportunity, and tried to demean or rob them?

8. Connie, the outwardly good and obedient daughter, eventually revealed the bitter resentment she held against her father and sister.

How able are we to distinguish the inside of a person's heart from outside appearances? What is required for any of us to know another or to know our true selves? Are you an elder sister? Do you resent a younger sister, assume she is the favorite? Have you ever done the right thing because it was expected of you, but inside you were silently resentful? Do you refuse to let sisters "out of the box"? Are you the unrewarded "good girl" in comparison to the "bad girl" who gets away with inappropriate behavior yet still seems to get more than her fair share? How are you like Connie? Do you know a Connie?

9. The father disregarded his own reputation and social standing to bring about reconciliation and unity between his children. He was as lavish with his love as Solana was with her inheritance. He was not willing for his daughter's servile mindset to negate their status as his children.

   Is it possible to assure children that love can be given equally but expressed differently? Do your children, friends, coworkers know that they are always welcome in your arms of forgiveness and acceptance? Are you as active as the father in your parental role? If your father in no way resembles the parabolic father, is it enough to consider God as your father?

10. This parable, perhaps more than any other, requires us to take an unflinching look in the mirror. God knows exactly what we look like and loves us as we are. God, portrayed as the ideal parent, accepts us in our youthful indiscretions, in our harsh judgmentalism, but desires our maturity.

Are you estranged from your physical or spiritual brothers and sisters? In what ways do you reflect your heavenly parent? Do you, do others, see you as a compassionate image of God?

Jesus' parable about the father paints a radically different portrait of God. "The divine father is revealed as the one who refuses to own us, demand our submission, or punish our rebellion. Rather, God is the one who respects our freedom, mourns our alienation, waits patiently for our return, and accepts our love as pure gift."[16]

Notes

Introduction

1. Spoken by the author's daughter; Gertrud Mueller Nelson, *Here All Dwell Free* (New York: Fawcett Columbine, 1991), p. 2.

2. For the entire story, read chapters 11 and 12 of 2 Samuel.

3. Jan Lambrecht, S.J. *Out of the Treasure, The Parables in the Gospel of Matthew* (Grand Rapids, MI: Peeters Press, William B. Eerdmans Publishing, 1998), p. 65.

The Image of Compassion

Chapter 1

1. The directive to love one's neighbor was present in Jewish writings at the time of Jesus: "Love the Lord and your neighbor. Have compassion on the poor and the weak." (T Iss 5:2). Pheme Perkins, *Hearing the Parables of Jesus* (New York: Paulist Press, 1981), p. 113.

2. Also known as the "Red or Bloody Way."

3. Robert Farrar Capon wrote: "I am disposed to take Jesus' postulation of such a descent as a parable in itself of his own downhill journey to his passion and death, and thus into the lastness, lostness, (leastness, littleness, and death) that he now sees as the heart of his saving work." *The Parables of Grace,* (Grand Rapids, MI: William B. Eerdmans Publishing, 1988), p. 64.

4. "The roads in Jesus' Palestine were very rudimentary and rough - the famous Roman road system had not yet been extended to Palestine. (Being attacked) was what everyone feared about the road in Jesus' day, and indeed what pilgrims and others have often feared since. (In the twelfth century the Crusader Order of Templars was founded to protect pilgrims travelling that way; in the nineteenth century pilgrims were given an escort of Turkish soldiers for the journey.)" David Wenham, *The Parables of Jesus* (Downers Grove, IL: Inter-Varsity Press, 1989), p. 155.

5. *The Great Sayings of Jesus: Proverbs, Parables and Prayers,* ed. John Drane (New York: St. Martin's Press, 1997), p. 60.

6. Jesus repeatedly warned about storing up treasures that could be stolen by thieves; he advised guarding against thieves in the night; he accused money changers in the temple of making his house of prayer a "den of robbers." At the end of his life, in a last-ditch effort to establish his guilt by association, Jesus was hung on a cross between two thieves.

7. Eta Linnemann, *Jesus of the Parables,* trans. by John Study (New York: Harper & Row Publishers, 1966), p. 54.

8. Wenham, p. 159.

9. Bernard Brandon Scott, *Hear Then the Parable* (Minneapolis, MN: Fortress Press, 1989), pp. 199-201.

10. Psalm 147:3; Isaiah 30:26.

11. "Inns were often rough-and-ready places, little more than a walled-off area with an open space in the centre for travellers' animals and porticoes round the sides under which visitors would sleep on the ground." Wenham, p. 157.

12. John R. Donahue, S.J., *The Gospel in Parable* (Minneapolis, MN: Fortress Press, 1989), p. 133.

13. Luke 6:27-28.

14. Matthew 5:43-44.

15. Robin Griffith-Jones, *The Four Witnesses: The Rebel, the Rabbi, the Chronicler, and the Mystic* (San Francisco: HarperSanFrancisco, 2000), p. 220.

16. Matthew 14:14; 15:32; Mark 1:41; 6:34; 8:2; Luke 7:13.

Chapter 2

1. John R. Donahue, S.J., *The Gospel in Parable* (Minneapolis, MN: Fortress Press, 1988), p. 132.

2. Donahue, p. 134.

3. Robert Farrar Capon, *The Parables of Grace* (Grand Rapids, MI: William B. Eerdmans Publishing, 1998), p. 66.

The Image of Forgiveness
Chapter 4

1. Brad H. Young, *The Parables - Jewish Tradition and Christian Interpretation* (Peabody, MA: Hendrickson Publishing, 1998), pp. 123-124.

2. Matthew 18:15-17.

3. Early Christian art depicted the Trinity in groupings of three, whether fruits, flowers, or animals; four was the number of fulfillment, as in four Evangelists, four gospels, four corners of the earth, four elements, four seasons, four Horsemen of the Apocalypse; seven was a sacred number, seen as perfection, creation, and as the union of God and humanity (3 + 4).

4. Leviticus 25:9-13. Jubilee comes from a Hebrew word meaning "ram's horn" or "trumpet."

5. In Genesis 4:24, Lamech looked for unlimited vengeance seventy times seven; in this parable, Jesus presented unlimited forgiveness seventy times seven.

6. Bernard Brandon Scott, *Hear Then the Parable* (Minneapolis, MN: Fortress Press, 1989), p. 268.

7. Luke 7:41-42; Matthew 20:1-16; 25:14-30; Luke 16:19-31; 19:11-27.

8. Luke 16:13-14.

9. The number ten was recognized as completion or perfection, as in the Ten Commandments.

10. For a historical perspective, the annual tax revenue for the combined provinces of Judaea, Idumea and Samaria was 600 talents. Herod the Great, by all means a rich king, had an annual income of 900 talents.

11. Some authors assert the original figure was 10,000 denarii, not talents, for a loan, not a debt. Ten thousand denarii was large enough to make immediate

payment difficult, but small enough to repay from the sale of property and possessions or contributions from family and friends, thus making the servant's plea for patience legitimate, yet maintaining disparity with one hundred denarii. Other authors ascertain that 10,000 talents was purposefully chosen to substantiate the line "as he could not pay," and to represent humanity's unpayable debt to God.

12. William R. Herzog II, *Parables as Subversive Speech* (Louisville, KY: Westminster John Knox Press, 1994), p. 140.

13. "The term for having compassion occurs a dozen times in the NT (in the Gospels only)." Apart from its use here and in Luke's parables of the Good Samaritan and Prodigal Son, the term is not used in reference to the emotions of persons. It is used in reference to God, expressing the divine compassion that is revealed in Jesus. In all three parables, the term is used in reference to persons who reflect divine compassion." Hultgren, p. 26.

14. William Barclay, *The Parables of Jesus* (Louisville, KY: Westminster John Knox Press, 1970), p. 87.

15. "Israel's Torah demanded that debt be forgiven every seven years. But some of the Pharisees had set up a legal fiction called *prozbul*, which enabled the holder of a debt to give the debt over to the courts. Because the debt was then no longer a personal debt, it did not have to be forgiven in the seventh year. One of the reasons given for this law was that creditors were not lending in the sixth year, since they knew that the next year they would have to forgive their loan. On the face of it, therefore, finding a way around debt forgiveness supposedly opened up credit. The end result, however, was the perpetuation of debt in the land, for such a law leads to increased incidence of foreclosure rather than forgiveness." Ch. 12: "Strange Neighbors and Risky Care" by Sylvia C. Keesmaat from *The Challenge of Jesus' Parables* ed. Richard N. Longenecker, (Grand Rapids, MI: William B. Eerdmans Publishing, 2000), p. 268.

16. John R. Donahue, S.J., *The Gospel in Parable* (Minneapolis, MN: Fortress Press, 1988), p. 77.

17. Herzog II, p. 146.

18. Donahue, p. 77.

19. Herzog II, pp. 146-147.

20. Matthew 5:7.

21. Matthew 6:9-13; Luke 11:1-4.

22. Longenecker, p. 265.

Chapter 5

1. Kathleen Norris, *Amazing Grace, A Vocabulary of Faith* (New York, NY: Riverhead Books, Penguin Putnam, 1998), p. 299.

2. Luke 16:14.

3. Luke 12:48.

4. William R. Herzog II, *Parables as Subversive Speech* (Louisville, KY: Westminster John Knox Press, 1994), p. 133.

5. Eta Linnemann, *Parables of Jesus* (London: SPCK, 1966), p. 78.

6. Robert Farrar Capon, *The Parables of Grace* (Grand Rapids, MI: William B. Eerdmans Publishing, 1988), p. 50.

7. Ch. 12: "Strange Neighbors and Risky Care" by Sylvia C. Keesmaat from *The Challenge of Jesus' Parables,* ed. Richard N. Longenecker, (Grand Rapids, MI: William B. Eerdmans Publishing, 2000), p. 264.

8. In 1998, Nicaragua, one of the world's poorest nations, owed creditors $6.1 billion, the highest per capita in the world. Debt-service payments of $254 million absorbed 52% of the government's revenue, 2½ times the country's spending on health and education combined. A child born in Nicaragua already owes $2,000, where the average yearly income is $390. Facts provided by *The Washington Post* and Jubilee 2000/USA.

The Image of Humility
Chapter 7

1. The approximately two million Jews who lived in first-century Palestine included three parties: Pharisees, Sadducees, and Essenes. The pacifist Essene sect, about 4000 in number, was devoted to purity in isolated, communal living. They took daily ritualistic baths, maintained a strict diet, wore plain clothes, owned no slaves, and generally abstained from wedlock. Sadducees, the smallest yet most educated and wealthiest group, adhered to the written law to the point of severity. They did not believe in angels, spirits, or an afterlife, but taught that freedom of will causes good, and evil results from human thoughtlessness. Pharisees held high standards of purity for Sabbath observance, cleanliness, and washing hands before meals. They shut non-Jews (Gentiles) out of governing councils, boycotted their businesses, and ostracized them from social affairs. Scribes, their scholarly experts, were devoted to the study and interpretation of the civil and religious law and determined their application to daily life. Their judgments became the oral law.

2. "Unclean" included those "smitten in his flesh, or paralyzed in his feet and hands, or lame, or blind, or deaf, or dumb, or smitten in his flesh with a visible blemish." Ch. 12: "Strange Neighbors and Risky Care" by Sylvia C. Keesmaat from *The Challenge of Jesus' Parables,* ed. Richard N. Longenecker (Grand Rapids, MI: William B. Eerdmans Publishing, 2000), pp. 263-285. Source (IQSa 2.11-12; trans. G. Vermes, *The Dead Sea Scrolls in English,* 2nd ed. (Harmondsworth, Middlesex: Penguin Books, 1975), p. 120.

3. Isaiah 25:6.

4. Luke 13:29.

5. Herod's banquet (Mark 6:21); dinner with Matthew (Matthew 9:10); Levi's banquet (Luke 5:29); wedding at Cana (John 2:1-11); Mary and Martha's (John 12:2); Jesus' food (John 4:31-34); washing before eating (Matthew 14:2, Mark 7:1-8; Luke 7:44-46; 11:37-41); feeding of 5,000 (Matthew 14:15-21); feeding of 4,000 (Matthew 15:32-38).

6. Luke 5:30; 7:33-34; 7:36-37; 8:55; 9:13; 10:8; 11:37-52; 12:22-29; 12:37; 17:6-10; 19:1-10; 22:13-38; 24:36-43.

7. Luke 15:2; Mark 2:16.

8. *Sacra Pagina Series, Volume 3, The Gospel of Luke,* Luke Timothy Johnson, ed. Daniel J. Harrington, S.J. (Collegeville, MN: Michael Glazier Book, The Liturgical Press, 1991), p. 225.

9. *A History of Private Life, From Pagan Rome to Byzantium,* ed. Paul Veyney (Cambridge, MA and London, England: Belknap Press of Harvard University Press, 1987), p.109.

10. *The New Interpreter's Bible,* Volume IX, (Nashville, TN: Abingdon Press, 1995), p. 286. Source: Pliny, the Younger Letters 2.6, in Pliny: Letters, trans. William Melmoth; Rev. W. M. L. Hutchinson, LCL, (Cambridge, Mass: Harvard University Press, 1951), pp. 109-111.

11. Matthew 23:6.

12. Author's paraphrase; see Mark 10:35-45 and Matthew 20:20-28.

13. John 13:21-26.

Chapter 8

1. Luke 1:52-53.

2. *Word Biblical Commentary,* ed. John Nolland, vol. 35B, Luke 9:21-18:34 (Dallas, TX: Word Books, 1993), p. 749.

3. *The Book of Common Prayer* (New York: Oxford University Press), p. 372.

Chapter 9

1. "Sisters" words and music by Dick Tunney and Melodie Tunney, 1993, BMG Songs, Inc./Dick and Mel Music (ASCAP). All rights reserved. Used by permission.

The Image of Grace
Chapter 10

1. F. Sommer, *The World's Greatest Short Story: A Study of Present-Day Significance of the Family Pattern of Life* (Oswega, KS: Carpenter Press, 1948).

2. Brad H. Young, *The Parables, Jewish Tradition and Christian Interpretation* (Peabody, MA: Hendrickson Publishers, 1998), p. 131.

3. William Barclay, *The Parables of Jesus* (originally published under the title *And Jesus Said* (Louisville, KY: Westminster John Knox Press, 1999), p. 187.

4. Robin Griffith-Jones, *The Four Witnesses: The Rebel, the Rabbi, the Chronicler and the Mystic* (San Francisco: Harper San Francisco, 2000), p. 221.

5. Young, p. 147.

6. Arland J. Hultgren, *The Parables of Jesus* (Grand Rapids, MI: William B. Eerdmans Publishing, 2000), p. 86.

7. Robert H. Stein, *An Introduction to the Parables of Jesus* (Philadelphia, PA: Westminster Press, 1981), p. 119.

8. John R. Donahue, S.J., *The Gospel in Parable* (Minneapolis, MN: Fortress Press, 1988), p. 153.

9. Henri J. M. Nouwen, *The Return of the Prodigal Son, A Meditation on Fathers, Brothers, and Sons* (Dallas, TX: Doubleday, 1992), p. 94.

10. Ibid. p. 96.

11. Thomas Cahill, *Desire of the Everlasting Hills—The World Before and After Jesus* (New York: Doubleday, 1999), p. 204.

12. Young, p. 154.

13. Hultgren, p. 79.

14. Barclay, p. 186.

15. Robert H. Stein, *An Introduction to the Parables of Jesus* (Philadelphia, PA: Westminster Press, 1981), pp. 121-122.

16. Philip Yancey, *Reaching for the Invisible God* (Grand Rapids, MI: Zondervan Publishing House, 2000), p. 45.

17. Ch. 9: "Parables on God's Love and Forgiveness" by Stephen C. Barton from *The Challenge of Jesus' Parables*, ed. Richard N. Longenecker (Grand Rapids, MI: William B. Eerdmans Publishing, 2000), p.209.

18. Cited in *Jesus and His Parables, Interpreting the Parables of Jesus Today*, ed. V. George Shillington, (Edinburgh, Scotland; T & T Clark, 1997), p. 156. (Ch. 9: *A Dysfunctional Family and Its Neighbours, The Parable of the Prodigal Son* by Richard L. Rohrbaugh, pp. 141-164.). This quote is footnoted: Kenneth E. Bailey, *Poet and Peasant*. Combined ed. (Grand Rapids, MI: William B. Eerdmans Publishing, 1983), p. 181.

19. Donahue, p. 155.

20. Robin Griffith-Jones, *The Four Witnesses: The Rebel, the Rabbi, the Chronicler, and the Mystic* (San Francisco: Harper San Francisco, 2000), pg. 221-222.

21. Longenecker, pp. 199-216.

Chapter 11

1. Henri J. M. Nouwen, *The Return of the Prodigal Son, A Meditation on Fathers, Brothers, and Sons* (Dallas, TX: Doubleday, 1992), p. 65.

2. Brad H. Young, *The Parables, Jewish Tradition and Christian Interpretation* (Peabody, MA: Hendrickson Publishers, 1998), p. 142.

3. "Prodigal Son" by Manfred Siebald, Johannes Gutenberg Universitat, Mainz, Germany and Leland Ryleen, Wheaton College from *The Great Sayings of Jesus, Proverbs, Parables and Prayers*, ed. John Drane (New York: St. Martin's, 1997), pp. 109-118.

4. John R. Donahue, S.J., *The Gospel in Parable* (Minneapolis, MN: Fortress Press, 1988), pg. 152-153.

5. F. F. Bruce, *Hard Sayings of Jesus* (Downers Grove, IL: InterVarsity Press, 1983), p. 170.

6. Brennan Manning, *The Signature of Jesus* (Portland, OR: Multnomah Press, 1992), p. 144.

7. Bernard Brandon Scott, *Hear Then the Parable* (Minneapolis, MN: Fortress Press, 1989), pp. 66-67.

8. 2 Corinthians 1: 3 (NIV).

9. Brennan Manning, *Ruthless Trust* (San Francisco: HarperSanFrancisco, 2000), p. 169.

Study Guide
The Image of Compassion

1. Thomas Cahill, *Desire of the Everlasting Hills* (New York: Doubleday, 1999), p. 185.

2. Joachim Jeremias, *The Parables of Jesus* (Upper-Saddle River, NJ: Prentice Hall, 1963), p. 202.

3. Cahill, p. 184.

4. Oswald Chambers, *My Utmost for His Highest* (Grand Rapids, MI: Discovery House Publishers, 1992).

5. John R. Donahue, S.J., *The Gospel in Parable* (Minneapolis, MN: Fortress Press, 1988), p. 133.

The Image of Forgiveness

6. Kathleen Norris, *Amazing Grace, A Vocabulary of Faith* (New York: Riverhead Books, Penguin Putnam, 1998), p. 299.

7. C. S. Lewis, *The Weight of Glory and Other Addresses,* revised and expanded edition. (New York: Macmillan, 1980).

The Image of Humility

8. John Ruskin, author, art critic, and social reformer, 1819-1900.

9. John Marshall Harlan, 1833-1911.

10. Chuck Colson, *Loving God* (Grand Rapids, MI: Zondervan Publishing House, 1983), p. 245.

The Image of Grace

11. John R. Donahue, S.J., *The Gospel in Parable* (Minneapolis, MN: Fortress Press, 1988), p. 159.

12. German drama *De Parabell van verlon Szohn,* 1527; Guilielmus Gnaphaeus' Latin *Acolastus,* 1528; Georgius Macropedius' *Asotus,* 1537; Jörg Wickram's *Schönes und evangelisches Spiel von dem verlorenen Sohn,* 1540; and Lope de Vega's *El hijo Pródigo,* 1604. Taken from *The Great Sayings of Jesus; Proverbs, Parables and Prayers,* ed. John Drane, (New York: St. Martin's, 1997), "Prodigal Son" written by Manfred Siebald, Johannes Gutenberg Universität, Mainz, Germany and Leland Ryken, Wheaton College, p. 110.

13. The Merchant of Venice, Love's Labour's Lost, Twelfth Night, Timon of Athens, As You Like It, Henry IV, King Leer, Comedy of Errors, Winter's Tale, Merry Wives of Windsor, The Two Gentlemen of Verona. Ibid., pp. 111.

14. Notably John Bunyan's *The Pilgrim's Progress,* Henry Fielding's *Joseph Andrews,* William Wordsworth's *Excursion,* Charles Dickens' *Martin Chuzzlewit,* George Eliot's *The Mill on the Floss,* John Steinbeck's *The Grapes of Wrath.* Characters of Thomas Hardy, William Butler Yeats, James Joyce all

quote lines from the original parable. Literary references are made by Geoffrey Chaucer, Daniel Defoe, Henry Fielding, Washington Irving, Edgar Allan Poe, Harriet Beecher Stowe, Graham Greene, Herman Melville, Mark Twain, Eugene O'Neill, Sinclair Lewis, Thomas Wolfe, and many others, affirming the universal appeal of this parable. Ibid., pp. 111-118.

15. Robert Browning, Christina Rossetti, Rudyard Kipling, André Gide, Rainer Maria Rilke, Frank Kafka, Ibid.

16. Sandra Schneiders, *Women and the Word* (New York: Paulist Press, 1986), p. 47.